Plant Feasts

Recipes for slow living in a fast-paced world

Frankie Paz

Plant Feasts

Recipes for slow living in a fast-paced world

Frankie Paz

NOURISH
EAT WELL, LIVE WELL

A love letter to the earth

PLANT FEASTS
Frankie Paz

First published in the UK and USA in 2024 by Nourish, an imprint of Watkins Media Limited Unit 11, Shepperton House, 89–93 Shepperton Road, London N1 3DF

enquiries@nourishbooks.com

Publisher: Fiona Robertson
Commissioning Editor: Ella Chappell
Project Editor: Brittany Willis
Copyeditor: Sophie Elleston
Head of Design: Karen Smith
Design Concept: Francesca Corsini
Production: Uzma Taj
Commissioned photography: Hannah Bodsworth
Food & Prop Stylist: Frankie Paz

A CIP record for this book is available from the British Library

ISBN: 978-1-84899-419-5 (Hardback)
ISBN: 978-1-84899-420-1 (eBook)

10 9 8 7 6 5 4 3 2 1

Typeset in Walburn, Cera and Benguiat Caslon
Printed in China

Publisher's note
While every care has been taken in compiling the recipes for this book, Watkins Media Limited, or any other persons who have been involved in working on this publication, cannot accept responsibility for any errors or omissions, inadvertent or not, that may be found in the recipes or text, nor for any problems that may arise as a result of preparing one of these recipes. If you are pregnant or breastfeeding or have any special dietary requirements or medical conditions, it is advisable to consult a medical professional before following any of the recipes contained in this book.

Notes on the recipes
Unless otherwise stated:
Use medium fruit and vegetables
Use fresh herbs, spices and chillies
Do not mix metric, imperial and US cup measurements:
1 tsp = 5ml 1 tbsp = 15ml 1 cup = 240ml

nourishbooks.com

Contents

INTRODUCTION

MY PLANT JOURNEY

A warm welcome.
This is me, Frankie Paz.

Like most journeys, mine came with twists and turns. Moments that shaped me, moments that shook me and moments that felt like they would literally break me. Yet it was also these very moments that were the making of me. If someone had told me two decades ago that it'll be plants that will help me through my hardest times and awaken parts of me I hadn't even realized I had inside, I would have rolled my eyes at them. Yet now I have been on this plant journey for 15 years, and it has taken me on some wild adventures. Plants have assisted me in opening my heart, overcoming drug addiction, feeling connected to nature, feeling more joy and finding balance, even in one of the biggest cities in the world.

Cooking with natural ingredients, which nourish deep and taste banging, is my passion. Creating simple plant-based dishes and sharing them with friends, lovers and strangers, while having honest conversations around the table (or in my case, on my home floor), has enabled me to connect deeper to nature, myself and those around me. Yep, sharing good food and conversation massively assisted my healing. Life shifts can actually be really simple.

I wasn't always this way, let's get this straight: I'm not a hippy, or from a posh house in the countryside, or born into vegetarianism. Nah, I'm just a city girl, with a gypsy heart that beats for freedom on all the levels. I was born in south London in 1989. We didn't have much money growing up, and my sister and I didn't have the most conventional childhood either. My mum worked all the hours under the sun as a cleaner to make sure we didn't go without. Yet she also made sure life was never dull. Our home was always open, full of students, lodgers and my mum's eccentric friends. It was a place of no judgement and no rules. It didn't matter what day you'd had, our home was a space to express, dance, eat, drink, support each other and celebrate life in all its madness. There was room for anyone and everyone. Every Friday "Reg the Veg" would rock up with all the bits that hadn't sold in his butchers and grocers that week, and he would sell them for a cheap price to mum. Some weeks she didn't have the money to pay him and he would say, "Don't worry, Jules, pay me next week." That's the thing about the working-class community, people look after each other.

I would help my mum with these home-cooked feasts, using only a few ingredients, inspired by how she seemed to create so much from almost nothing. The party was always centred around food, and everyone always got fed, even if we didn't end up eating till 10pm. It was fun but, in all honesty, I always craved "normality". My mum was never gonna be normal though – her own mother was a trapeze artist in the circus. For my mum, life is a celebration and an adventure. As I got older, I realized that there is no "normal"; that real beauty is in the weird and wonderful. My passion for cooking and love for community started at home with my mum. She taught me one of the biggest lessons: just because society puts you in a box, doesn't mean you have to stay in it. In fact, burn the fucking box!

My father died when I was 12 after substance abuse took its toll on him. As you can imagine, it rocked my world. While other twelve-year-olds were thinking about puberty, I was contemplating the meaning of life. From as young as I can remember, I never felt like I fitted in. I existed somewhere between the modern world and the ancient world, and I felt my path was to find a balance between the two. Little did I know then that food and ceremony would be that bridge. When my dad passed, I became a lot closer to his mum, Nana B. She is now 97 years

FRANKIE & NANA B

old and has been vegan for 60 years. She has taught meditation and was a homoeopathic nurse in World War II. I have fond memories of the contrast between my mum and nan one Christmas. While my mum was cooking turkey, my vegan Nana B was freeing our pet rabbits and guinea pigs. It was wild. Nana B's passion was always, and still is, plants, and she has so much knowledge about the plant world. If we were ill as children, she would do reflexology on us and give us herbal potions. She paved the way for many, and some would say she is a wisdom keeper. An inspiration indeed. In all honesty, I thought she was pretty strange growing up, regularly talking about "honouring the earth", "breathing deep" and "wild swimming". But she planted a seed in me. I just needed to go far away to finally see her wisdom: that in the end nature does have all we need.

I left home at a fairly young age and was following in the same footsteps as my father – self-destruction on London's party scene. Of course it was fun, I was exploring all realms and I met my tribe who had the same passion for freedom. But as time went on, I became addicted to the scene and the drugs. I was burning out, working intense hours as a hairdresser and then partying through the night, pretty much every night. I knew things had gotten bad when one of my best friends told my drug dealer to stop selling to me. And yet, I was more concerned about where I was gonna get my supply from than my friend's worries. I knew deep down that I couldn't carry on, that I had to take a different path to the one my father took.

I left everything I knew aged 20 and followed a call from the beat of the jungle. I fell in love with a man I met in the Amazon and moved to his home country of Colombia, where I stayed for many years. It was wild. We had barely any money, existing hand to mouth; but this is when I learned to truly trust the universe. At 23, I was married and immersing myself in a new land, with a new language.

We lived in the mountains on the border of a jungle where the land met the sea, where the indigenous people believed the world had begun. I became more and more connected to nature and my spirit.

I simplified everything and ate only fruits and vegetables, nuts and seeds, and cut out all caffeine and gluten. It was an extreme contrast to my previous lifestyle. Over time, my body detoxified and I started to really, really feel. It was a lot, and it was scary. I learned that to embrace my darkness, my shadow, is the only way to live a connected life. And in fact, it had only been me holding myself back, with the limiting stories I was telling myself.

I learned from various communities and their elders. They taught me that each and every thing we consume in this world is an energy exchange. For these people, life is a ceremony, and how they interacted with nature is ceremonial. My whole life transformed. I was building fires, learning that nature was very much alive, and that I was lucky to be alive. I had so much space to think and feel. It was very confronting and different from the world I had left behind, but I felt extreme peace living this simple life. All that I had known to be true about myself had been taken away, and what was left was revealed. It was beautiful, it was fucking hard, it was a rediscovery, it was a return to love.

With my passion for cooking, every day I would experiment in the kitchen. We had one rustic but beautiful stove, and so my plant creations had to be simple. After many years abusing my body, I knew that it was time to heal it. My then husband was unenthusiastic about vegan food, as were others in the community, so I knew I had to make my creations taste really good. Over time they loved my meals, and soon many of them started to enjoy mainly plant-based food. Through cooking, I was channelling my art as well as nourishing my body. It was so healing for me. I still had much to learn about the wide range of fruits and vegetables available, but I was discovering more every day. I realized cooking with plants on a daily basis was not only sustaining me physically, but it was also helping me to learn and connect with nature and myself. Food was becoming my ceremony and was bringing me so much joy.

The elders in the community would talk of the earth being alive and refer to her as Mother. They would laugh at my city ways and how I would reply "really?" to everything. I remember the first week I arrived, I sat around the fire and told my story of addiction. They were shocked and asked, "Why would you put poison in yourself? You are part of Mother Earth, and what you do to you, you do to her." I had never thought about it in this way. In London everything was about separation; here everything was about connection. As time passed, I started to see that the people in this community saw no disconnection between nature and themselves. Nature was an extension of them. They celebrated the sun and honoured the moon. Slowly over time I started to feel the same. It was

almost like I was reawakening this innate connection to the natural world inside me that had been lost. Of course emotions came up, as did cravings. It was hard, I was unravelling, and there was a lot of pain. But I would sit with the plants and learn from them. Nature was holding me. What no longer served me, I gave back to nature. Life was simple. There were no mobile phones. We would pray to the fire daily and share stories. The stories soothed me, made me laugh and gave me hope. I realized that many of the things they talked about had similarities to my grandma's teachings. They were more radical; they were living in the jungle, guided by the wind and the stars, and my Nana B was living in a city. But over time I started to see that maybe fusing the ancient natural world with the modern world was the key to finding more balance in my life ... even in a city.

My then husband and I then lived with various communities in Peru and Ecuador. One of these was a raw food community, and it was here I mastered sauces, found my passion for the blender and pretty much lived off salads. I learned to balance flavour, and to make banging desserts using only natural, unprocessed ingredients.

It was at that point I realized that I wasn't running any more. I was softening and my heart was opening. In fact, I was surprised at how much love was inside me. We didn't have much money. Sometimes we would use a cut-up can with lighter fluid as a stove for cooking. I cut hair along the way, sometimes on the streets, and my then husband sold his handcrafted jewellery. We were basically hustling any way we could, and what we did have we shared with those around us. I started to see that when I brought more ceremony into my life, everything just flowed better. I felt more connected to myself. Growing up, I was taught that ceremony meant a big event, but I've since learned to find ceremony in the smallest things. Waking up mindfully in the morning, preparing a home-cooked meal, making a potion, going for a walk in nature and even telling stories. In the communities we stayed with, I would watch how strangers shared their own stories of love and pain, telling them with such vulnerability and openness. It was medicine. As one person opened up, it was an invitation for others to share their stories in an expressive way, an invitation for deeper conversation, deeper connection. Often I and others who heard the stories could relate to the emotion on some level, and that would touch us all and leave us inspired for days. My grandma would always talk of storytelling from our ancestors, but now I was seeing that our own personal stories can connect us, and that we can see each other in what is shared.

I could have stayed in South America. On some level it was paradise, but I knew I had to return to London in order to see if I really had overcome my addictions. And I knew it was time to go home and connect to my own roots.

I went home to London and worked my arse off, managing to save enough money to study raw food cuisine in LA, California. I learned lots, but I couldn't align with what I was being taught. We were using natural foods, but with so many complicated processes and techniques. Yeah, the flavours were great, but it wasn't simple, and some of the recipes took hours or even days. Who has time to milk an almond for three days? I was used to living in tune with the source of my ingredients and working with what was available locally. Here it felt like we were glamourizing nature, and on some level this felt more disconnecting. It just reinstated my belief that plant-based food should connect you to nature and be easy and accessible.

When I returned to London, I studied lots. I struggled to relate to some plant-based recipe books. Some of the content was super spiritual or proposing just living off green juices. I was all about eating plants and making them taste good, spending a bit of time in the kitchen, and a bit of time foraging. But most importantly, I was about finding balance in a city – fusing my jungle life with my life in Hackney and staying true to me.

At this time, not many people even knew what veganism was. I found the vegan food scene was very small and pretty expensive. It seemed that if you wanted to eat healthy vegan food, you basically needed to be rich, and that eating food made with plants and connecting to nature was unattainable for the majority. My then husband couldn't understand how people were putting a price on spirituality. So, I created raw food supper clubs called Moody Mango with an emphasis on connection – not just to the food, but to the community. I kept the price affordable, with an intention for people to meet others who might be different but who were on a similar journey with food, and to show how good plant dishes that nourish deep can taste. The supper clubs took off. I was preparing the food from a tiny bedsit, and over time it was just too much for me. Yeah, I was starting to make money but, like all things, as they get bigger, it's hard to maintain your original intention. I now do my events on my boat, inviting only small groups at a time, and calling them ceremonial supper clubs. We learn about the land, share stories, read poems and feast on plants. The suppers have become a place where strangers become friends, and the city fades away. Nobody talks about what job they do or their relationship status, but there is an emphasis on how we feel and what we

think about the world. Sometimes the conversations are uncomfortable, but we learn from each other, and we get comfortable with the uncomfortable.

It took a while to settle back into London life after many years away. I travelled some more but mostly remained grounded in my home city. I studied modern psychology, matrix reimprinting and reiki. I experienced many different teachings, workshops and events: healing sessions, sound healings, leaf and bone readings, chats with pirates, druid teachings, voice sessions, archetype work, losing myself on the dance floor, breathwork, exploring different states of consciousness, and learning the basics of astrology. I was also working on a deep level with plant medicines, shamans, ceremony and rituals. Yet what consistently assisted me deeply was creating and sharing banging plant-based dishes while listening to people's stories being told around the table.

Nowadays, I'm outside as much as possible, and when I'm in nature I feel most myself. I still live on a boat in Hackney and connect to the elements daily. I love the city and all the magic it offers. I still hold ceremonial supper clubs and host circles on the boat where we come together on full moons and new moons to drink potions and honour nature and ourselves. We call these moon jams. I spend more time with my grandma,

asking her questions about foraging and listening to her stories. But most of the time you'll find me making potions or plant dishes on my boat along the marshes. Or dancing until sunrise. I can do both!

Plant Feasts isn't a normal cookbook. This is my journey of returning to love on all the levels, infused with the wisdom of elders, with a few stories in between. Sometimes I feel we have forgotten that food can be a bridge, an invitation. With mental health problems at a peak, food made with whole plants can be one way we can look after our bodies. As we connect to nature, we connect to ourselves. In a nutshell, I'm about bringing more balance into a fast-paced life, and being honest with who we really are. This book is inspired by 15 years of my

purely gluten-free plant-based life. I have been eating and developing all the recipes in this book for many years. Some of these recipes I created when I lived in the jungle and mountains of Colombia, some when I lived in communities, some in squats, some just pottering around London on my boat and some while catering for boujie events around the world.

So many things have shaped who I am and the life I live. My grandmother's wisdom, finding sobriety, love, death, heartbreak, divorce, sex, travel, wild swimming, taking time off to be still, late-night conversations with friends and strangers, laughing so hard my belly hurts, crying so much my face hurts (you know those deep, deep cries!).

It's not always easy healing yourself and breaking away from destructive patterns. It can be really, really uncomfortable when you know you have to change things. But it's worth it, every little bit of it! My life is proof of this. So give it a go, make a dish, make a potion and share a story of how you really feel. Create a ceremony for yourself, and if you want to, share it with friends, with lovers, even with strangers.

I hope the recipes and musings in the book give you as much joy as they have me!

Big love, Frankie x

WHAT IS FOOD AND CEREMONY?

When I talk about "food and ceremony" people often ask, well, what do you even mean by that? The word ceremony can put people off, like I'm gonna get all religious on them. For me, there's nothing religious about food and ceremony; it's actually all about bringing real presence to what we are doing, a sacredness if you like. It's about taking it back to the days before mobile phones, when we connected over mealtimes, telling stories around the dinner table. This has been done all over the world for thousands of years, yet, somehow, we have forgotten this innate way to tell stories and bring presence to our meals.

Over the last 15 years, while creating and serving plant-based foods, I've seen that the real magic happens when we bring intention to preparing our food. Food and ceremony for me includes taking time to make dishes look beautiful, with ingredients that align with nature and, in return, with ourselves; giving thanks to the hands that harvested and sowed the seeds; taking a moment to breathe before we dive into the dishes we have created; sitting with others to share our stories while we share dishes; even creating art with plants. These seemingly small simple acts might seem insignificant. But let me tell you: they can transform lives. I know because I'm living proof of it.

The world moves way too fast, and we rarely have time to pause. These small and easy rituals allow me to slow the fuck down and just give myself a minute. To pop some flowers on my dish and give thanks to the Earth. It doesn't have to take lots of time either. I love cooking, but I like to spend more time around the dinner table sharing stories and laughing.

Even if you are making food for one, there is something powerful about making a meal for yourself and really being present for that time of nourishing your body, about taking the time to cook yourself something with love, grown from the earth. My grandma would say that eating plants and creating dishes that fuel you on all the levels is the ultimate act of self-love.

Living in Colombia, my mum's passion for community, my nan's influence and all the people I ever cooked for are what inspired me to create the ceremonial supper clubs, where people feel seen and heard. What better way to eat more plants and bring ceremony back to food?

So how do we bring ceremony back to food?

Here are some ideas you might want to consider:

* No phones
* Taking the time to make your dish look beautiful
* Storytelling around the dinner table, focusing on having deeper conversations. This can be inspired by thought-provoking questions I've provided on page 23
* Bigging up the people that harvested the food and Mother Earth for providing. If this feels a little too much, then simply take a moment to appreciate what it took to bring the food to your table
* Reading poems
* Listening or singing to music
* Lighting candles

As you read through this book and read the recipes and my stories, I invite you to give it a go: take time to light a candle, to give thanks, to make your food beautiful for yourself. Sometimes it is the smallest acts that make the biggest difference.

STORIES AROUND THE TABLE

There is something beautiful about coming together for food. Plant feasts and deeper conversations are where it's at for me. So many times, I have sat around a table or on the floor with a stranger, connecting over a meal, having conversations that left me inspired for days, opening parts of me, sometimes even challenging me and questioning why I even feel this way.

Sharing our stories that are raw and real requires a level of vulnerability and openness that we often find scary. Yet, the magic of vulnerability is that as you open, I see myself in you, and as I open, you start to see yourself in me too. Maybe sharing plant dishes and what we believe is not as radical as it seems? What if we just took a moment and didn't hide? I don't care what you do for a living; I want to know who you are, not what you do. We have become so used to defining ourselves by our work, that we have forgotten who we are. I think we have forgotten the wisdom that lives deep inside us.

My Nana B worries that my generation has lost its way, and that we suffer with anxiety, depression and other mental health issues because we have swapped the storytelling for TV and our mobiles. She says people didn't feel so alone back in her day. She tells me it's all about a good question, connecting to nature, love and play. When I was living alongside tribes in the jungle in South America, we would come together for breakfast, lunch and dinner and we would talk about our day and tell our stories. The elders would tell us stories of Mother Earth and the gods that lived in the mountains. They shared that "We are the children of the Earth and we have to look after each other". It was the first time I had heard stories passed on like that.

The world is full of people. I lived in one of the busiest cities in the world, but still felt lonely at times. Then I realized what was missing: community. I'm not the only one who has felt this way. We can be in the same room as someone else and feel alone. Yet by having deeper conversations around the dinner table, we can feel seen, and connected. There is nothing more powerful than being seen and heard. I have seen how being vulnerable and speaking your story can lead to a deeper connection with others. When I talk about community, I'm not talking about a community of just like-minded people, but also of people who challenge me. I think it's important to hear different beliefs and different perspectives from all walks of life. I love it. It makes me have more compassion for others and helps me not to stay rigid in my ways of thinking. And when I learn that someone who I think is completely

different from me has at times felt the same as me, that brings a deep feeling of connection.

Storytelling and sharing are the most important parts of my ceremonial supper clubs. You never know what the topic of conversation might be, but one thing's for sure – it's never boring. I recall one particular powerful evening where guests arrived as strangers and parted as friends. As I started passing the dishes around the table, plates full of vibrant plant-based delights, I started explaining about nettles and what our ancestors would do with this medicinal plant. Then someone chimed in: "Do you feel connected to your ancestors?" "I do," I replied, "It's only in recent years I have started to remember what runs through my bloodline. Yet so much knowledge has been forgotten over time."

This sparked a conversation about heritage. Even though we were a table of strangers on a boat somewhere in Hackney, each person's heritage was somewhere different: India, Colombia, Ghana, London, Ireland. A mix of culture and stories. That's why I love London, this city I call home.

Each person spoke of how they connected to their ancestors. Some people hadn't thought about it too much. Then a man in the corner spoke up. He shared his sense of aloneness, and how he had felt lost for so long until he started to connect with his ancestors

and heritage. It was then that he regained his sense of connection because it was something greater than himself. He felt less alone and felt like he belonged. Then a woman from Colombia spoke about her results from a DNA test saying that, in fact, she was 15 per cent Colombian and the rest Scottish. For her whole life she had identified with her Colombian roots and now she felt so confused. Questions of "Who am I? Who are my ancestors? Am I gonna have to wear a kilt now?" raced through her mind. As we all shared our stories, we all had a longing to learn more about our ancestors, in the hope that through them we would understand ourselves more. That evening, we connected over a yearning to discover more.

Then someone chuckled and added, "You know what I think. We may not know much about our ancestors, or some of us even where we come from. But what we do know is that we come from the earth, all of us, and maybe we connect to that and learn."

The room smiled as the words hit us all.

I invite you to switch up the questions at your next meal. See what you can learn about from the person sitting next to you ...

QUESTIONS FOR THE DINNER TABLE

Here are a few questions I've used at my supper clubs and dinners
with friends and even family. You may want to give them a try.

1. What makes your heart sing?

2. When was the last time you laughed so hard you wet yourself?

3. What does this season mean to you?

4. What do you think about death?

5. If money didn't matter, what would you be doing?

6. Is there a time where you experienced absolute stillness and how did that feel for you?

7. When was the last time you fell in love?

8. How do you connect to nature?

9. How do you connect to yourself?

10. If you could name a storm, what would you call it and why?

11. When was the last time you allowed yourself to feel sad?

12. Do you fully let go in sex?

13. Are you an observer of life or a participant?

14. Where are you not showing up in your life?

15. Do you know much, if anything, about your ancestors?

16. Do you believe in life after death?

17. Do you believe in magic, and if so, how do you bring magic into your daily life?

18. What's your favourite song? How does it make you feel? Where does it take you to? Can you hum it?

19. Have you ever experienced having no money? If so, what was that like for you?

20. Have you ever got somewhere only to realize that you were happier before?

21. When you reach the age of 80, what do you think you'll smile at the most?

22. Have you felt anxious before and what do you do when you feel it present?

23. What advice would your 90-year-old self give you? What advice would your 18-year-old self tell you?

WHY PLANTS?

There's no denying that if you eat more plants, you will feel the benefits. Our bodies need a varied diet that is rich in colour and full of vitamins and minerals in order to thrive. I have yet to meet someone who says they don't feel better from adding more fruits and vegetables into their daily life. And as you feel better, you start to create better choices in your life and, in turn, the planet. When we incorporate more plants into our lives, no matter where we're at, things start to happen. We start to feel more alive, and that can infiltrate into all aspects of our lives. I could tell you a million reasons why we should all eat more plants. I have read hundreds of books supporting the science about thriving on a plant-based diet. But for me, it wasn't the science that got me into this plant life, it was how it made me feel; that was evidence enough on its own.

I've also witnessed how sharing plant-based food not only connects us to the people around the table, but also connects us to the earth. For me, eating plants is one way I connect with nature daily. When I say plants, I am talking about fruits, vegetables, herbs, nuts and seeds – food that comes directly from the earth. As we prepare the plants in the kitchen, we are working directly with nature every day, and over time that deepens our connection to it. As we consume more plants, soon enough our body starts to awaken to this innate connection we have with the natural world.

When I was a child, Nana B would tell me regularly that nature is all we need. In the 90s, we went to her local restaurant called The Harvester and my nan asked what she could eat as a vegan. I saw the waiter look at her like, what the hell is a vegan? And me, well, I was sat with my head in my hands, embarrassed. Let me tell you this: nobody knew what a fucking vegan was in the 90s, and I didn't want my nan to keep banging on about it either. I found the courage and piped up and told the waiter, "She just eats a lot of plants as natural as possible."

What I realized in that moment is that it doesn't matter what label you give yourself, as long as you are eating lots of plants. You could be vegan, plant-based, keto, or meat and two veg. Today I see that a wholesome plant-based diet is keeping my nan thriving at 97 years old. Her skin is great, and her mind is sharper than mine. She puts it all down to eating more plants, breathing deep and being in the garden. She says we are all so busy searching for facts to try and prove that something works, that we get lost in the "whys". But the feeling behind it all is

what is most important. She would tell me often to take inspiration from our ancestors. We have lost our connection to our ancestors and all their wisdom, yet it is through plants we can remember how strong our connection to the earth is. Plants have been here long before humans, and our ancestors survived just fine eating them for thousands of years; we've just got better at cooking and seasoning them.

When I was in South America, I learned that plants are our oldest ancestors and until we take the time to get to know them, we will never fully understand ourselves. It is the plants that heal and feed us, lift our spirits, and connect us deeper to our own nature. They saw plants as medicine, each one offering something different. Each fruit and vegetable was treated with so much respect, and honoured with an energy exchange.

We all have a connection to the plant world; without plants we can't live. Yet it seems that we have forgotten just how strong that connection is. We have swapped connection for convenience. When we take the time to align with the plants in our lives, learn what energy they bring and how they can

support us, we can use them to enhance our lives with their magical properties. Our innate connection to the natural world reawakens. I believe we can do this through cooking and bringing ceremony to food, and sharing that food with strangers, family and friends or even just ourselves.

It's like anything: the more you focus on something, the more you attract it. As we eat a diet with an abundance of fruits and vegetables, we increasingly understand that these types of foods are vital for us to thrive. Nature gives us what we need – water, oxygen, sunshine, plants – and we have a choice as to whether we want to connect to it and work with it. So basically what I'm saying is just give it a go, wherever you are on your journey, just eat more plants, whatever that means for you. Start with one dish and build on that. Channel that inner alchemist you have inside you. Follow your intuition and see how you feel over time. I know your body will crave it, because in order for us to feel nourished we have to give our body nourishing foods. Give your body a diet rich in many things and it will support you in all the ways you need it to.

This is the ultimate act of self-love.

SEASONS AND SEASONAL FOOD

I'm not militant about only eating local seasonal foods, but giving seasonal foods more focus has been a great way for me to connect to the land around me, to connect to nature and to make recipes more cost-effective too. A lot of my recipes were created when I lived in the jungle, using only what was in season there. Imported ingredients were a rarity, so sourcing local seasonal produce was essential. These recipes have evolved to be a fusion of fruit, vegetables and nuts from faraway lands, along with my much-loved ingredients from here in the UK.

What thrives on the earth at certain times of the year will indeed make you thrive too. My grandma often asks me, "Francesca, are you paying attention to nature, are you watching what is growing around you? What gifts is nature gifting you in this very moment?" I wonder, if we all asked ourselves these questions and took the time to sit with them often, would we look at nature differently? I believe that as we start to pay attention to the nature around us, wherever we are, we can't help but connect to it more.

Back in my grandma's day, there would be a small window when each vegetable was available. She would have to be really present for what was growing at the time, otherwise, boom, she would miss the moment. My grandma's generation had to work with what they had. They had to care for the land in order to make sure they could survive. But things have changed. Our connection to the plants and seasons has been lost. We can get whatever we want, when we want, provided we have the funds. It's something we have to actively relearn, but something magical happens when we eat more in sync with what is growing around us. When produce is picked at its optimal time, it is full of nutrients, including vitamins and minerals, and the taste is SOOOO much better!

I grew up in south London, where there were only city farms: one pig, a few chickens, a couple of sheep, and only eggs for sale. These weren't farms that grew food. I later had to learn what actually grew on the land where I was born. The first time I saw a celeriac as an adult, I thought it looked like a beautiful alien. I had no idea what to do with it. I tried it raw at first, but it wasn't great. Then I roasted it and added wild garlic pesto and it was banging. This vegetable that seemed otherworldly to me is now a staple in my recipes.

As years went on, I spent more time outside learning about what grows at different times of the year. I would go to city projects that grew seasonal food. I loved getting creative with the variety of produce that would arrive in local veg box deliveries. I started looking at supermarkets and seeing what seasonal offers there were. And then I found the confidence to start foraging (see page 38). I also love going down to the markets for end-of-day deals. I hate waste, so if there's a box of overripe mangoes on discount, I'll take it and turn them into a chutney, then create a dish with a seasonal vegetable to go with it. It's about finding a balance that works for you.

Nowadays, it's all about the seasons for me. Not just the produce it gifts us, but learning how to work in harmony with each season to optimize our mood and energy. By working with spring, summer, autumn and winter, we can use the gifts they offer us – the fruits and vegetables available at each point in the year give us exactly what our body and mind need at that time. My grandma was

right. As I started to learn about what was growing around me, I started to feel more connected to the seasons and the land; I started to reawaken this innate connection I believe our ancestors had to the seasons, cycles and plants. In fact, I believe we all have this innate connection inside – its just a matter of reawakening it.

In my early twenties I was on the go all the time, working hard cutting hair, hustling to make ends meet, then partying even harder. I felt like society expected this of me. Yet as I worked more with the seasons, I saw that this didn't have to be the way. The seasons reflected how I could be. Winter took pauses and so could I. I learned to harness my increased energy in summer, and used winter as a time for rest and reflection, which helps me to create more balance and harmony in my own life. Spring is a time when it's all about bloom, when I think about what I want to bring to life in my own life. Autumn is a time of letting go of what no longer serves me. Seeing all the colours change reminds me I'm not meant to stay the same.

SOLSTICES AND EQUINOXES

The solstices and equinoxes are important transitions in the natural world, a pivotal point where the seasons are changing. They have been celebrated by many cultures around the world for thousands of years, including mine in the UK, and are an integral part of our pagan past. My grandma says that the change of seasons are a really important point for us all too, when nature really speaks to us and the land changes quite dramatically.

When we use nature as a guide, it can assist us in our personal change.

In my supper clubs or circles we gather on my boat and talk about how the season is affecting us individually. We learn about the plants that are growing right now and celebrate their nutritional and medicinal qualities. As I hear about how certain times of year affect each person individually, I see I can relate to it in some way.

SPRING EQUINOX
AROUND 20 MARCH

The first sign of spring for me is when the snowdrops appear and not long after that the wild garlic comes out. That's when pesto season commences. It's a good time to put flowers in the house and on our plates to lift our energy after the cold winter, a reminder of the awakening happening around and inside us. As more colour appears in nature around us, we can reflect this in the dishes we prepare. It's the season of bitter plants, which can help cleanse and detox the liver after a long winter of eating heavier foods.

Spring is all about reawakening, rebirth and balance. Late spring is when is when stone fruits come into season. It's a great time to set our intentions for summer and the year ahead. A time to think about what seeds we want to sow in our internal world, and if we have a garden, or like me a boat roof, what seeds we want to sow in the physical world.

Some questions I ask myself as spring approaches:

* What am I letting go of in my life?
* What do I need to make room for?
* What seeds am I planting for the year ahead?
* Where do I need to bring more balance in my life?

Artichokes, asparagus, beetroots/beets, broad/fava beans, cabbages, carrots, chicory/Belgian endive, elderflowers, kale, leeks, lemons, lettuce, morel mushrooms, new potatoes, parsnips, purple sprouting broccoli, peas, radishes, rhubarb, rocket/arugula, samphire, spinach, spring/collard greens, spring/scallions onions, sorrel, watercress, wild garlic

SUMMER SOLSTICE
AROUND 21 JUNE

The sun is at its peak and so are we. There is an abundance of fruit and vegetables. Summer is all about fire, creation and sexual energy. Life can feel quite fast-paced, but if we channel this energy, it's a great time to make the seeds we sowed in spring come to life. It is a time to celebrate the strength and power of the sun and the richness of the earth.

As summer approaches, I consider:

* Where do I need to bring more balance in my life?
* Where can I bring more creativity and passion?
* Where can I show up more in my life?

While the land is in full bloom, eating lots of fruit and salad with a high water content will help replenish us in the summer heat, gifting our bodies exactly what they need.

Asparagus, apples, apricots, aubergines/eggplants, baby carrots, beetroot/beets, blackberries, blackcurrants, blueberries, broad/ fava beans, broccoli, cherries, chicory/ Belgian endive, chillies, courgettes/ zucchini, cucumbers, damsons, edible flowers, fennel, garlic, gooseberries, greengages, green beans, kohlrabi, lettuce, loganberries, mangetout/ snow peas, marrows, mushrooms, new potatoes, peaches, peas, peppers, plums, potatoes, pumpkins, radishes, redcurrants, rocket/arugula, runner beans, samphire, sorrel, spring/ collard greens, spring onions/scallions, strawberries, summer squash, sweetcorn, Swiss chard, tayberries, tomatoes, turnips, watercress

AUTUMN EQUINOX
AROUND 23 SEPTEMBER

For me, the transition to autumn can be hard. I cling on to the warmth and vibrancy of summer. But my grandma often reminds me of how much better life is when we stop holding on to things, when we let go of it as effortlessly as a tree lets go of its leaves; even though the branch has supported it for so long, it gracefully lets go. Nature starts to slow down and I take this as an invitation to slow down too. It's time to tell the world to jog on for a bit, I've socialized enough.

As the leaves fall, I take pauses to figure out:

* What am I grateful for from the summer?
* What do I want to shed?
* Is there anything that I have been avoiding over the fiery summer?

The autumnal season gives us warm shades of oranges and browns. The land is starting to get damp, there's a cool evening breeze and wild mushroom foraging season starts soon. As the days get shorter and nights longer, I transition to cooking soups and stews with warm spices. Root vegetables grown under the earth are a great way to stay grounded through this transition.

Apples, aubergines/eggplants, beetroots/beets, blackberries, broccoli, butternut squash, carrots, cauliflowers, celeriac, celery, chard, chicory/Belgian endive, chillies, courgettes/zucchini, cucumbers, damsons, elderberries, fennel, figs, garlic, greengages, kale, kohlrabi, leeks, lettuce, mangetout/snow peas, marrows, onions, pears, peas, peppers, plums, potatoes, pumpkins, quinces, rocket/arugula, radishes, raspberries, redcurrants, runner beans, samphire, spinach, spring/collard greens, spring onions/scallions, sorrel, summer squash, sweetcorn, swedes/rutabaga, sweet potatoes, Swiss chard, tomatoes, turnips

WINTER SOLSTICE
AROUND 21 DECEMBER

As the days turn darker and colder and the trees become bare, it's a great time to create, get cozy and to reflect on the year that has passed. Winter is a time of slowing right down. Less doing, more being. A time for creating and building our inner foundation while taking lots of rest, and building fires to remember the sun – for even in the darkest of nights there is still light – and celebrate its eventual return, for no matter how dark it gets the light will always return. It's time to prepare for a new cycle, a time where even in such darkness we go in and build our strength for the brighter days ahead.

Eat greens and roots to keep grounded in this time. Bitter veg like kale help to look after the kidneys and liver. Lots of stews to stay warm and potions to keep the spirits high.

As nature pauses, I follow her lead and ask myself:

* What is the darkness teaching me?
* What truths do I need to face?
* Where do I need to soften?
* What do I want to bring in with this new cycle?

Apples, brussels sprouts, cauliflowers, chestnuts, chicory/ Belgian endive, clementines, cranberries, Jerusalem artichokes, kale, leeks, onions, parsnips, pears, pomegranates, potatoes, pumpkins, purple sprouting broccoli, quinces, red cabbage, rhubarb, Savoy cabbage, spring onions/scallions, squash, swedes/rutabaga, Swiss chard, turnips

EATING ORGANIC

I was once told by a friend in the Andes that the organic farmers are the real caretakers of the Earth. They use less chemicals and look after the Earth's soil. From that point on I started to eat more organic food whenever I could. It can be expensive and I didn't always have the option. However, my friend gave me some great advice with regards to this. He said that if I couldn't afford to eat organic all the time, then I should at least try to eat organic fruit and veg that have thin skins, as these usually don't contain high amounts of residual pesticides.

Here's a short list that you might try:

* Apples
* Berries
* Celery
* Cherries
* Cucumbers
* Grapes
* Kale, collard and mustard greens
* Nectarines
* Peaches
* Pears
* Peppers
* Spinach
* Tomatoes

FORAGING

Foraging can bring more balance into our lives, getting us outside and connecting deeply with the plants on our doorstep. Picking food straight from the earth, in its natural timing, is nourishing on so many levels. When the plant is in season and gifting us with its presence, that is when it's packed full of vitamins. It's rare we can eat food straight from the earth but when it comes to foraging that's exactly what we can do. No industrial farmers, no long-distance exports, just your hands in the soil, then making something with these earthly delights. I'm gonna be honest here though: I love foraging and all the magic it gives, and I love making and creating things with my plant finds; however, the foraging missions that take ages are really not my jam. I don't have time to milk a rosehip for two days. So the recipes you'll find in this book use plants that are pretty easy to find and easy to incorporate into a busy life. I like to call it "weaving the ancient with the new".

Even in the biggest of cities there are things to forage. Some are perhaps a little more obvious, like apples and blackberries. Others we have been told are weeds, and to stay away from, like nettles or mugwort. I have learned over time that maybe those plants we were taught to fear could be the very things that can assist us to a deeper connection to ourselves. These so-called weeds are medicinal and thankfully grow right under our feet, popping up in abundance in rural areas and even in the busiest of cities. Full of vitamins and minerals, they give our bodies exactly what they need when the season gifts them. And the best thing is, it's free food and available for anyone who wants to take a moment out of the man-made world and reconnect with the ancient world.

When we think of a city, we don't typically think of nature. It's not surprising that people struggle to believe we can forage for edible plants in cities such as London or New York. Yet nature is always around us, gifting us, it's just that sometimes it's not so obvious. No matter what destruction we seem to throw at the plant world, it always finds a way to grow. You just gotta pay attention.

I never knew much about foraging growing up. As I learned, I reawakened my connection to my local plants, and as I started to learn more about what I was able to eat from the land around me, I started to learn more about the cycles of nature around me. It made me feel more aligned, not only with plants, but with my own cycles too.

Foraging brings a presence to nature like nothing else. When you're walking and searching for a particular plant, you become totally in the moment, engaging with all your senses. Wild garlic is my favourite. It's in season for only a couple of months, so if I'm not present with nature and its ever-changing seasons, I know I'll miss my chance and have to wait a whole year for the next cycle of these incredible plants.

I am forever learning something new about what plants we can eat, and learning what is edible right outside my little boat. Every time I'm on a walk, wherever I am, I'm checking out all the plants, what's coming into life, what's in season, and how I can make it into something delicious and easy to prepare. Food picked straight up is not only gonna elevate my creations but give me some deep nourishment too.

When I first embarked on my foraging journey, I asked my grandmother, "Where do I start? There are so many plants!" She said, "Start with what catches your eye, what jumps out at you, what speaks to you." So, I would go for walks, wherever I was and see what plant I would connect with.

It all started with mugwort for me. I picked it, sat with it, studied it, read about it, hung it up in my boat, drank it for one month, smoked it. I even put it under my pillow to invoke more visions in my dreams and wrote poetry about it.

It was a love story, mugwort and me, my initiation into the foraging world.

I was told by my Nana B that mugwort has the energy of an old woman who wants to give you an embrace, and that it can assist in dream work. I learned that it's psychoactive, which means it affects moods, awareness and feelings. I learned that our ancestors used it in ceremonies. This was a game changer. There was no need to look to other lands for my plants. I had powerful medicinal plants here on my doorstep. These days I regularly mix rosemary and mugwort and give it as an offering to the fire or burn it as incense.

I would tell my Nana B all this new information I had learned online and from books, and she would say, "That's wonderful, dear. But you don't learn about the natural world inside, not in a classroom. You must learn outside. You must learn about the plants like you would a human; take time to get to know them, hear their stories." So, I dedicate every month to a plant that I'm drawn to or that has caught my eye, and I go deeper with it. This is how I develop my foraging skills, all led by the plant, with a bit of book study and internet research thrown in.

On a walk in the jungle many moons ago, I was told that we have the wisdom of the plants inside us, we have just forgotten the way. That's why it feels so good to connect with nature: it's in our DNA.

When we do, we just reawaken what we already know. During the pandemic, I saw a huge shift with more people foraging. People had the space to reassess their lives. We were advised not to leave our homes, yet with time on our hands, it was trees and nature that we craved. I had many conversations with people while out foraging. Many said that as they were learning about what they could eat, they were reconnecting with nature and the land around them.

I remember when I was having a hard time in my marriage. I tried many things to make it work but our journey was coming to an end, although I couldn't see it. I was on the phone to my grandmother while I was walking in the marshes. I told her this was my month of nettles. She said, "Oh, this is exciting." I rolled my eyes. She said, "Sit with the nettles, Francesca, they will gift you and tell you what you need to know." I got off the phone a bit annoyed. I was hoping she was going to tell me some facts, or some profound metaphor for life. But I was so in my head with worry about what I should do next that I gave it go. I went to Hackney marshes and I "sat" with the nettles. My mind was going through so many thoughts, and then I picked them with my bare hands. One leaf stung me and I jumped. I definitely wasn't in my head any more. My grandmother was right, though: it was a reminder that it was time to put some

boundaries in my relationship. Not long after that, my husband and I separated. It may sound strange to some, but nettles really showed me that even in the deepest of loves, I needed to have healthy boundaries to honour myself.

I guess what I am saying is, just get outside, start noticing what is growing in season, what looks most alive. Go with friends. It's so much fun when we learn together; it can be a really good way of changing a dynamic within a friendship. Swap gossip for plant facts. Or go for walks alone – for me that is like meditation. Just me and the plant world. Go and chat to other foragers and ask them what they're looking for. Yep, I'm that person, and I've made many new friends this way. There are some great apps that can help you to identify foraging delights too if you live in an area where there aren't other foragers around.

As well as learning what grows around Hackney marshes and in the city, I love going away to other parts of the country, exploring and seeing what is in abundance in other areas. When I pick something wild and make something with it, I feel that I'm nourishing my mind, body and spirit. It's like a ceremony, an energy exchange between nature and myself. I'm honouring the plant, taking only what I need, picking it conscientiously.

Just a note: take only what you can see in abundance.

Here are some foods you can forage for:

NETTLES
LATE MARCH–APRIL AND JULY–EARLY OCTOBER

I go foraging for nettles when I know I need nutrients. They are full of vitamin C and packed full of iron – they have more vitamins and minerals than spinach! And, let's face it, nettles are everywhere. My grandmother says they are also really good for compost. They are a plant that gives in so many ways. I love nettles in soups, stews and pestos, even risotto. When I would normally use spinach, I use nettles. Sometimes when I have a soup on the stove, I pop outside and pick a few to add to the pot to make it extra nourishing. They have an earthy taste that's similar to other greens.

They are best picked when they are tender; you only ever want to pick their young leaves from the top of the plant. Use gloves and make sure they're not by the path or pavement, as a dog may have peed on them. Once wilted they won't sting, so it's always best to either blanch them in hot water or leave them out to dry.

You can make nettle tea, which is great for inflammation, pain and eczema, as well as prostate health. Nettle is also good for cleansing the kidneys, body and blood.

In times past, it was known as the plant of protection, and in Norse mythology it was connected to Thor, the God of Thunder, and the element of fire. To invoke protection, throw some nettles into the fire. Nettles have also been likened to the energy of the wise woman. Just as the wise woman represents balance, the nettle's double leaves also reflect this. Nettles are a reminder to take only what we need and to have boundaries.

THREE-CORNERED LEEK
JANUARY–APRIL

I walked past these beauties for years before I realized that you can eat them. They look very similar to bluebells but they're white. The flowers can be used in salads, soups or stews, or to brighten any dish, and the roots can be used as you'd use onion or garlic. They have a similar taste to chives or spring onions/scallions and they can be eaten raw or cooked.

They're called three-cornered leeks because the stem has three corners. You can find these beauties along pavements, towpaths, parks, field edges, woodland edges ... they pop up all over the city. The stems start to show in January, but they are at their fattest and juiciest in Febuary and March. The flowers then gift their presence from early spring.

They help lower cholesterol and blood pressure and can be a tonic to the digestive system. They have antibacterial and anti-fungal properties.

WILD GARLIC
MID-FEBRUARY–APRIL

When wild garlic comes out is when the foraging season starts for me. These versatile leaves can be used for pestos, stews, salads and even wild garlic salt! You can't help but catch the strong distinctive smell of garlic as you walk in the woods. The leaves are long and a distinctive bright green. However, please make sure that the leaves smell like garlic before you pick them, as they can be mixed up with Lily of the Valley, a poisonous doppelganger. As the season ends, the white flowers will come out and you can eat not only the flowers but also the seeds. I call these seeds "garlic capers" and they can be used in a salad for that extra bit of punch.

Wild garlic is said to aid renewal and purification, helping to purify the blood with its detoxification properties. Some also believe that this plant helps to shake off the dozy haze of winter. In the past, people would carry the leaves around in their pocket to ward off the flu.

WILD FENNEL
MAY–SEPTEMBER

The flowers of this delicious plant come out in summer and are bright yellow like the sun. I use the yellow flowers and leaves for salads or to season a potato dish, or I chop them up and put them in a salad dressing. They have a slight aniseed taste, so when you're picking them, you will smell this beautiful aroma.

Pick the leaves when young and green. They look a little like dill. You can find this beautiful wild plant by the sides of roads, in ditches and near the coast. It likes dry places.

It's an ancient plant with a long history of being used as food. It's great to blend with chamomile and mint in a tea, which is very refreshing and calming and great for heartburn and digestion.

WILD GARLIC SALT

Serves: 4 Time: 10 minutes + 1 hour drying in the oven or 48 hours drying naturally

This is how I preserve all the wild garlic goodness. Wild garlic gifts us with its presence for only a couple of months, but with this salt I get to enjoy the taste for the whole year, if not longer. I also give it as a present to people, and they love it. A simple gift for food lovers. A salt that elevates any dish.

I use this salt on salads all the time. In fact, I use it on everything. It's also a great conversation starter ... "Why is your salt green?!"

WHAT YOU'LL NEED
Blender
Baking sheet

INGREDIENTS
200g/7oz wild garlic leaves
800g/1lb 12oz sea salt

METHOD
Blend the wild garlic leaves in a blender until they become a smooth paste. Add 250g/9oz of the salt and blend for a couple of seconds. Transfer the mixture to a baking sheet, mix the rest of the salt in, making sure everything is well combined, then spread out evenly.

Leave in a warm spot for 2 days until it's really dry. It might need less time; it all depends how warm and dry your home is. Transfer to a container with a lid and store in the cupboard.

If you're like me and live on a boat or somewhere where it can be a bit damp at times, then pop the baking sheet in the oven at 50°C/120°F for 15 minutes. Give the salt a stir, then turn the oven off and leave it in there for 30 minutes.

Notes...

Over the year, the taste will fade slightly, as will the colour. You can use any salt, but I like to use sea salt, as I feel the white salt really absorbs the green colour of the wild garlic, making it look super witchy and wild!

BLACKBERRIES AND RASPBERRIES
AUGUST UNTIL THE FIRST FROST

When I see blackberries and raspberries I know there isn't long left of summer. You can find them in most hedgerows. I freeze them and use in smoothies and jams, add them to porridge or mix them into cakes.

Both berries are said to be connected to the heart. Raspberries are said to be a sign of fertility. The leaves when used for tea can help to strengthen and tone the uterus and prepare the body for labour, and this magical leaf eases PMS pains, too.

Blackberries are full of vitamin C. Every time I pick them I remember my grandmother's words: "Our hunter-gatherer ancestors used to do this thousands of years ago. Brambles have deep roots and picking blackberries is an invitation to connect to your own roots." They are one of the strongest plants of this land. You know they are ripe when they pop in your mouth with juiciness.

APPLES
LATE AUGUST–NOVEMBER

When money was tight, I would go foraging for all kinds of things. A popular choice for me was apples to make stewed apples to pimp up my porridge. You can find apples everywhere: in cities, woodlands, gardens, parks and even along the streets. You know they are ready to be picked when they come away from the branch complete with the stalk. If you are gathering apples from the floor, make sure you check for wasps and worms. Wild apples are full of nutrients, which are great for digestion and aid the liver. Apples are associated with magic, paradise and the gift of knowledge. Foraging apples is known as "scrumping" and has been done for hundreds of years. It is said that to share love is to share an apple, so if you share half of your apple with the one you love, passion will grow between you and be as fruitful as a tree grown from an apple pip.

MUGWORT
LATE MARCH–OCTOBER

This plant is pure magic! You don't have to go to the heart of the Amazon jungle to encounter a mind-altering plant because this little beauty can be found all over the world and is native to the UK. Mugwort is considered a mild psychoactive herb, promoting a state of sedation and euphoria. It tends to grow in forested areas and gardens, along roadsides and around the coast. You can use it to either cleanse spaces like in incense or drink it in a tea. It is said to be great for digestion, calming nerves, the liver and boosting your immune system.

Many ancient cultures smoked mugwort to promote vivid dreams and connect with intuition, using it in their rituals and ceremonies. This plant is great if you are trying to wean off the nicotine as it can be mixed with tobacco, gradually decreasing your dose until your body's need for nicotine has been reduced enough to stop smoking entirely. For ganja smokers it can bring a dreamy energy combined. This herb is a light smoke with a pleasant, slightly sweet flavor, use the dried leaves.

In the past, our ancestors would hang the herb over the door to keep away evil spirits. The best time to harvest the leaves, flowers and roots is in the summer, while spring is the best time to harvest the young shoots.

MAKING YOUR FOOD BEAUTIFUL

I'm all about making dishes beautiful, but it doesn't need to be about perfection. It's about making art with plants. It's about having fun and taking a few moments before you serve your meal to create beauty with nature's bounty.

We live in such a fast-paced world where, often, we don't pay attention to what we are eating. Yet, if a dish is beautiful, it can bring us right to the present moment, helping us to get out of our heads and into our hearts.

When you see a visually-pleasing plate in front of you, full of colour and perhaps decorated with a few flowers, you can't help but smile to yourself before you get stuck in. Without realizing it, you have taken a moment to acknowledge the beauty of the plants before you, a moment to connect with what you are eating. A moment to give gratitude to Mother Earth and all her bounty.

Taking time to make your food beautiful is like a meditation using plants. It doesn't need to be expensive. Believe it or not, you don't need to be rich to make things look beautiful; in fact, you don't need much at all. Plant dishes are already full of colour. By simply adding a few flowers and a sprinkle of herbs, you can elevate your plate to the next level.

For me, presenting dishes is like poetry, inspired by Mother Earth. It's one of my favourite things to do. People talk about how beautiful they look. They ask questions about what is being served, which creates connection around the table, but also we all acknowledge the plants. This offers an opportunity for a kind of ceremony between the plants on the table and ourselves.

Creating with plants can encourage change in us. I have had days where I can't be bothered, but when I make that little bit of time to create with plants, it can really shift my mood, and even at times get me out of a deep funk. There are days when I wake up and I feel flat or lazy. Then, I step outside, pick a daisy, or sprinkle some dried rose petals on my porridge, and straight away my food, and life in general, looks that little bit brighter. You might be reading this and feeling like you aren't that creative. Let me tell you that we are all creative in our own way. When I say beautiful, I mean whatever is beautiful to you. Sometimes I look at my food and see a beautiful mess that is rustic, wild or even a little chaotic. Other times, I look at my food and I think it looks pretty elegant. Ultimately, beautiful is whatever I believe it to be on that day and what reflects my mood. So, make it fun. Make it playful without the idea of perfectionism; in fact, fuck perfectionism! Making my dishes beautiful in my own way has been great for invoking more creativity into my everyday life.

When I lived with a community in the Colombian jungle, I saw creation in everything they did. I would watch Alma (the main cook) plate up the food. Everything was colourful and decorated with flowers, served on leaves. The food always looked so alive. I remember her telling me that nature has everything we need, we don't need anything else. She would often say, "Take the time to serve your food with love. Take pride in it."

Alma was right. Her wise words have supported me through those times in my life when I was broke (like, searching for 20 pence down the sofa broke, or having to ask the market stalls to give me what they were throwing out broke). Even in those hard times, I always took the time to make my food look beautiful, even if I was eating porridge for breakfast, lunch and dinner, or just rice and some overripe tomatoes. When I look back, it was a way of showing love to myself even in the harder times, that even in a harsh world I can still give myself a meal that nourishes and tastes and looks delicious.

Here are a few simple notes on how I make my food look beautiful.

THE RULE OF THREE

A main rule I follow is the rule of thirds. In nature things come in threes. My grandma would talk of this often: mother, father, child. Earth, sky, water. Life, death, rebirth. We seem to be attracted to threes. So, when I plate things up you'll notice that I plate in threes. Three flowers or three sweet potatoes.

If I have a large dish and want more than three tomatoes, I will always use odd numbers. Why? Because, to my mind, odd things just look better; there is a beauty in odd, something that's visually pleasing to the eye. The number three is mirrored all around in nature. If you look at most leaves, they will be in odd numbers, our eyes like it, as they have seen it so often and recognize odd numbers.

STACKING

I love to layer foods. Loaded sweet potatoes stacked with all the different toppings or balanced roots with nourishing grains. Layers and layers of goodness. Just try and make sure you see all the different layers so you get a range of colours. Also, creating height with your dishes can really make them look beautiful.

COLOURS

Use a range of contrasting colours, and make sure you can see all the colours, especially when stacking. Even the simplest of dishes, like a bowl of rice, can be taken to the next level by cutting up some fresh herbs and sprinkling them on top. Not only will they give lots of flavour, the white of the rice and green of the herbs will look amazing together.

NUTS AND SEEDS

I use chopped nuts and seeds to add texture and more volume to the plate – I call it a sprinkle of bits. Not only does it make the dish look beautiful, but it gives a surprise burst of flavour with a crunch.

FRESH HERBS

I always have fresh herbs on top of the dish, not only because of flavour, but because they can bring a delicate touch to a plate.

SAUCES

I use a squeezy bottle for drizzling sauces, so they look beautiful rather than simply dolloped on top. I can be quite heavy-handed, so adding an elegant drizzle has taught me to be a bit gentler with my dishes – and probably in my life too. Also, a good flick of sauce using a teaspoon can really elevate a dessert. It gives it an artful paint-splash effect, which can look pretty cool.

FLOWERS

You can't help but see beauty when you see flowers on your plate.

To be honest, I use flowers a lot, especially those that can be easily found outdoors. Learning about the different edible flowers can be a great way to get outside and learn about the land around you. It's also a very inexpensive way to dress up your dishes.

Edible flowers that can be found easily in the UK:

* Borage flowers
* Calendula flowers
* Chive flowers
* Clover flowers
* Daisies (yep, daisies are everywhere, just make sure they are clean)
* Dandelion flowers
* Gorge flowers, aka the kissing flowers (available in winter)
* Three-cornered leek flowers (great for salads and salty dishes)
* Pansies
* Rosemary flowers
* Violets
* Wild garlic flowers
* Yarrow flowers

I also have dried flowers that I use a lot on desserts, smoothie bowls and porridge. I usually take them from my grandmother's garden as I know they are organic and have no nasty chemicals on them. I dry them out over the log burner and then break them up to add a sprinkle here and there. These are perfect to use in the winter when there aren't as many flowers around or to pop on top of a potion.

You see, when you decorate things with the beauty of the earth, it connects you deeper to it.

KITCHEN APPLIANCES FOR SMALL SPACES

I have made food in all sorts of places – from the boujiest of kitchens with every apparatus known to man, to the smallest of rooms where I'm using tiles as chopping boards on the floor and heating porridge on an old cut-up can with lighter fluid and bricks. This has taught me that you can create nourishing food with almost nothing and from the smallest of spaces (I have catered for supper clubs of 80 people in a tiny bedsit in Hackney!) but, of course, having some basic appliances does indeed help and speed things up. Don't get me wrong, I love cooking, but I'm all about spending less time in the kitchen so I can spend more time at the table sharing with friends and strangers.

I live on a boat so I don't have lots of kitchen space, but over the years I have narrowed my essential kitchen appliances down to these. You can buy them second hand which makes it less expensive.

* **FOOD PROCESSOR** – I use a food processor for pestos and energy balls; sometimes, if it has a shredding blade, I'll use that for cutting veg too. Also great for hummus.

* **GLASS JARS** – I use glass jars to drink out of rather than cups because I often break cups on the boat! I also use them to store sauces and chutneys. Super versatile.

* **HIGH-SPEED BLENDER** – I use this for smoothies, nut butters, sauces and turning grains into flours. The most expensive thing that I couldn't live without is a good blender. I once had a blender that was powered by a bicycle! I really had to work hard for that morning smoothie …

* **JUICER** – there are two main types of juicers: macerating and centrifugal. A macerating juicer is slower and you have to cut the fruit and veg into smaller pieces. They are great for green juices, as they work well with herbs and can get the juice out of anything. A centrifugal juicer is more powerful, easier to clean and

great for citrus. This is the juicer I have, because it's easier and quicker.

* **JULIENNE PEELER** – this is amazing and a really quick way to prepare vegetables. Plus, it's super small, so can fit into any drawer.

* **KNIFE** – a good sharp knife will make you whizz around the kitchen. I don't have a massive range of kitchen knives, just two good ones. One large and one small.

* **MANDOLIN SLICER** – great for slicing your fruits and veg into thin slices. For people who consume plants on a daily basis, a good mandolin will minimize your prep time and allow you to speedily slice, shave and grate vegetables. I use mine all the time, especially with purple cabbage.

* **MEASURING CUPS** – yep, it's an American thing and I'm often asked, why cups? For me, it makes it so much easier in the kitchen. I'm dyslexic, so too many numbers throw me. Scooping a cup of flour feels so much easier than weighing and transferring it into a bowl.

* **MEASURING SPOONS** – get some proper measuring spoons. They make things a bit more exact and recipes wayyy easier to follow.

* **MICROPLANE** – great for mincing ginger and garlic and for zesting citrus fruits. You can even grate a nut on this smart little gadget.

* **SPIRALIZER** – it may be a bit bulky but I couldn't live without my spiralizer. If you're a person that likes to cook for the masses, then this is a great tool, especially for veg noodle dishes.

* **SQUEEZY BOTTLES** – these help to make your dishes look fancy … I like to say lazy fancy. Great to smother your food elegantly.

THE PANTRY

For me, every herb and ingredient has an untold story waiting to be discovered. Each ingredient that is grown in the earth comes with its own unique energy, and as we combine these wonders and create recipes, we create new stories and magic, magic that soothes and nourishes our lives and bodies.

Nothing excites me more than a pantry – all that magic in one room! I don't actually have a pantry, but one day I will. In the meantime, I have a corner of the boat filled with loads of herbs, spices and staple ingredients that I have collected over the years, and these are the things that I have on hand to create any recipe or potion.

I have spent years studying the plants and the magic they contain. My grandma and various elders from Colombia and other parts of South America have told me each plant has a nutritional value and an energetic essence too. What I mean by that is the energy it can bring to you on a spirit level. Some may call it old wives' tales. Yet maybe they are the tales we have forgotten. Maybe they are the tales that are waiting to be remembered. These foods are full of vitamins and minerals that not only heal and nourish deeply but also empower our bodies. Every plant has magic inside that wants to work with our

bodies and minds to bring us more into balance. As we learn the intricacies of the plant world, we learn more about the earth and, in return, ourselves; we learn what can assist in making our mind, body and spirit return to more harmony.

As you start to incorporate more of these plants, don't be surprised when your body starts to crave certain ones each day. Your body will connect with what it needs. It's important to follow your body's intuition. Ultimately for me it's how it makes me feel, rather than the why. I always make sure I have my favourites on hand, so I can reach for them anytime I need to.

POWER PLANTS

NOTE: an adaptogen is a plant that works where your body needs it.

* **ASHWAGANDHA** – adaptogen, thyroid supporter, stress reliever
A plant that has been used all over the world for thousands of years. It is a root that calms the nerves. It also aids in thyroid function and assists in lifting depression. It helps sleep and overall vitality. It is a plant that meets you where you're at as it can give you energy and at the same time calm you down.

* **CACAO POWDER** – mood booster, joy activator, metabolism booster, heart soother

This plant is all joy, an aphrodisiac and heart opener. It assists you in opening your heart as well as helps to release endorphins. It gives you energy and lifts your mood. Low in caffeine but still gives lots of energy. They say this beautiful plant is food of the gods.

* **CHAGA MUSHROOM POWDER** – adaptogen, immune booster, inflammation tamer

A universe-in-one mushroom known as the ultimate health booster. It is said to slow the ageing process with its anti-inflammatory cell-strengthening power. It also protects against DNA damage. Very nutrient dense. Tastes earthy.

* **CHIA SEEDS** – digestive aid, detoxifier, brain activator

These magical little seeds are full of omega 3 fatty acids, proteins, fibre and antioxidants. They help to detox the body and nourish skin, hair and the internal organs. These little seeds are powerful. They have been used by indigenous communities in Peru for years to help with stamina and are believed to assist in moving mountains.

* **CHICORY/BELGIAN ENDIVE ROOT POWDER** – digestive aid, heart soother

This plant belongs to the dandelion family and it looks after the liver. It is earthy and malty in flavour. It's perfect for potions. My grandma tells me that in the UK we used to drink this in the mornings before coffee was imported. It looks after the stomach and aids digestive health. They say it's a protector of the spirit.

* **MACA POWDER** – adaptogen, hormone balancer, energy booster

This Peruvian root helps the body to adapt to stress and anxiety. It is a tonic to boost the endocrine system. It delivers abundant energy and mental stamina and heightens the libido. If you want more sex and love making in your life, this is the plant for you!

* **REISHI MUSHROOM POWDER** – immune and energy booster

This little mushroom is one of the best immune boosters in the world. Bold statement but I'll own it. They call it the shroom of immortality. It nourishes the heart and reawakens the spirit, creating feelings of centeredness. It can soothe allergies, protect the liver and support brain function. It has a slight bitter, earthy taste.

SPICES AND ACCENTS

* **ALLSPICE** – mood lifter, digestive aid
Helps to improve circulation and mood. It also helps to increase brain stamina and is great for digestion. It is said that it also stimulates healing and assists in prayers for good luck.

* **APPLE CIDER VINEGAR** – energizer and body balancer
This versatile vinegar is alkalizing, cleansing and energizing. It can be used for all sorts of things from sauces to potions. It was used to treat war wounds, as well as counter mushroom poisoning. I sometimes take it in a little water in the morning, as it helps to balance my body's pH level and maintain my gut health.

* **BLACK PEPPER** – digestive aid, immune booster
This warming spice boosts the immune system, nourishes the kidneys and activates the digestion. I use it in milky potions and meals as it brings an earthiness and complements other herbs. Used for medicine and spells back in the day. It was called the king of spices. We used to offer it to the gods.

* **GROUND CARDAMOM AND PODS** – joy enhancer, digestive aid
This anti-inflammatory and anti-bacterial spice is rich in flavour, lifts the mood and is considered an aphrodisiac. It goes well with earthy meals.

* **CAYENNE PEPPER** – detoxifier, digestive aid, metabolism booster
Assists in detoxing and is a circulation activator. Its rich spice increases the pulse of the lymphatic and digestive rhythms. It can heat the body and inspire cleansing and radiance. They say this spice makes you smile and can ignite passion.

* **CINNAMON** – body balancer
This fragrant spice balances blood sugar, tames inflammation and soothes the spirit. Its cozy and fragrant warming energy was said to be connected to the sun and it was often used in love spells.

* **CUMIN SEEDS/GROUND CUMIN** – digestive aid, immune booster
This spice is my favourite because it elevates everything. It helps digestion and has antioxidant properties. This rich, warm, earthy spice enhances the savoury flavour of plants. It is also said to symbolize love and commitment. In the past, it was placed in the pockets of couples before the wedding.

* **GARLIC POWDER/GARLIC** – immune booster and detoxifier
A great antibacterial that assists in balancing the blood. This is perfect for winter colds as it protects the immune

system. Used in ancient times to ward off evil. A great all-rounder for adding a bit of spice to your dish, and protecting your immune system.

GINGER – digestive aid, detoxifier
They say this powerful anti-inflammatory root can speed inner creative fire and add passion to an existing relationship. It also helps to strengthen your immune system and combat nausea. Perfect for potions and to give that earthy, spicy fire to a dish.

MUSTARD SEEDS – immune booster
These tiny aromatic seeds are rich in selenium and are great for maintaining bone strength. They can be used to relieve toothache and pain in the gums. Their mild, nutty flavour carries the essence of horseradish. These seeds are also known as the seed of faith.

NORI – detoxifier and alkalizer
These beautiful leaves from sea forests boost metabolism, balance hormones and soothe the thyroid. They are a good source of iron and are full of flavour. Perfect for making wraps with raw veggies when in a rush.

NUTMEG – immune booster, digestive aid
An ancient pain reliever, and good for the blood. It was used for incense and is said to possess magical qualities to ward off evil. Perfect for potions and sweet and savoury dishes.

NUTRITIONAL YEAST
Gives a nutty and cheesy flavour to dishes and is a good source of vitamin B12.

*   **PAPRIKA** – inflammation tamer, immune booster
Paprika is made from ground peppers. It helps prevent inflammation and improves blood sugar levels. Rich in vitamin C and other antioxidants. You can buy sweet, smoked or spicy.

*   **ROSE PETALS** – joy activator and heart soother
These have been consumed for centuries to sooth the heart and mind during stressful situations. They are also an aphrodisiac and support metabolism. Have them on hand to add to a potion or to decorate a dish and invoke some love and passion.

*   **SALT** – balancer
This universal spice is an electrolyte. Good salt is important. It brings balance to the body and brings out flavours with food. I use sea salt from Cornwall or pink Himalayan salt. Salt has always been used to protect: from preserving foods, to warding off evil spirits.

*   **VANILLA EXTRACT** – aphrodisiac, stress reliever
This potent, aromatic antioxidant soothes the nervous system, relieving stress, and is an ancient aphrodisiac.

FATS

NOTE: soaking nuts makes them easier to digest and less acidic in the body.

*   **ALMONDS** – beauty food
Almonds look after the heart and help blood flow. I use them a lot to complement earthy dishes and they are great in desserts. In addition, almond oil is good for the skin and hair. This sweet nut is said to be connected to the vulva and fertility, thus the almond is an awakener to the womb.

*   **CASHEW NUTS** – brain activator, beauty food
Full of minerals and good fats, cashews are great for the brain, bones and mental health. I use cashews a lot to make creamy sauces.

*   **COCONUT OIL AND COCONUT BUTTER** – beauty food, brain activator
Coconut supports the thyroid, balances blood sugar and helps to eliminate toxins. It is antiviral and anti-fungal and full of healthy fats. If I have a cut in my mouth, I will gargle on coconut oil to help it heal. Coconut butter is the fat of coconut and I use it a lot in raw cakes.

* **FLAXSEEDS** – brain activator, inflammation tamer
Ground flaxseeds help to balance blood sugar as well as being a beautifier and a body cleanser. These tiny seeds are powerful and can be used to bind dishes instead of eggs.

* **MACADAMIA NUTS** – beauty food, digestive aid, brain activator
This nut is alkalizing, sweet and smooth, perfect for cakes and dips. Great for the skin and the gut. Macadamias are said to invoke creativity and imagination.

* **OLIVE OIL** – brain activator, beauty food, metabolism booster
This energizing and brain-powering oil is rich in antioxidants and great for hormone balance. If you can, buy organic olive oil. This ancient oil is known for wisdom and kings were anointed with it.

* **SESAME SEEDS AND TAHINI** – plant protein, beauty food, brain activator
These seeds are an antioxidant, full of protein and B vitamins. They say this seed is the seed of immortality and when the gods met to create the world, they drank wine made from sesame seeds. Tahini is made from ground sesame seeds and is great for dips and sauces. I tend to use light tahini, made from hulled sesame seeds, as it's smoother and creamier.

* **SUNFLOWER SEEDS** – beauty food, energy food
These seeds assist in lowering blood sugar levels and are full of magnesium and potassium. They say giving sunflower seeds to someone means that they will be loyal to you. They are associated with the sun, fertility and confidence.

* **WALNUTS** – brain activator, joy enhancer, hormone balancer
I was told the reason these little nuts look like a brain is because they are great for brain health! Full of omega 3 fatty acids, which help reduce oxidative stress in the brain and lift your mood. Connected to the god of the sky and thunder.

STAPLE GRAINS

*   **OATS – grounding, support emotions and digestion, lower cholesterol**
I use this versatile grain for baking and desserts. Amazing for eczema: soak oats in warm water, then apply to affected area. They are also great for constipation.

*   **QUINOA – balances blood sugar, can improve gut health**
An ancient seed from the Andes. It has a nutty flavour and is full of plant protein and fibre. It is called the holy seed and they say it has a universe inside, that it was gifted from the stars. Rinse before use to help remove any bitterness. Great for salads and soups. Can be used in offerings for ceremonies and rituals.

*   **RICE – energy enhancer**
This ancient grain is gluten free and has been a dietary staple for many cultures around the world for thousands of years. It is used in ceremonies and rituals too. I use white rice more than brown because it cooks quicker, and I always try to buy organic rice.

SWEETENERS

AGAVE SYRUP – supports mental health
Taken from the sap of the agave cactus plant, agave syrup is high in vitamin K, which can help with mental health. I love using this to sweeten as it adapts to any dish. It is said that this plant was found to comfort the soul of those who had lost someone dear to them.

* COCONUT SUGAR – supports blood sugar balance
This sweetener is made from the sap of the coconut and is low glycaemic, which means you don't get those sweet highs and then crash. It has a caramel kind of taste.

* DATES – support digestion
Dates are full of nutrients. They are good for digestion and boost energy. They are dense and give a caramel taste and depth to any dish.

* MAPLE SYRUP – supports the nervous system
The sap from the maple tree is very sweet and delicious on pancakes, as well as on earthy savoury dishes. It looks after the nervous system because it contains zinc, magnesium and potassium.

Notes...

I get asked a lot why I never use lids on my pots when I cook. Personally, I love to see what I'm cooking, how the food transforms and its process while I'm creating (I love a process). I feel it helps me connect more to the plants, appreciate their beauty and makes me a better cook. So none of my recipes will mention a lid, unless I'm cooking quinoa or rice as they need to steam at the end.

BREAKFAST

When your body is asleep, it repairs itself, recharges. In the morning, you want to wake it up gently, give it foods that feel good, fuel it with plants that nourish on all levels. When I wake up, I make lemon tea and read poetry. Then I make a juice or a smoothie. My grandma always tells me that how you start your day impacts the rest of it. So, start it with love and nourishment.

CARDAMOM BANANA BREAD

Serves: 10   Time: 50 minutes

When the pandemic hit, my friends and I started making this as part of our weekly routine. It is said that vanilla and cardamom are natural aphrodisiacs; looking back, I think we just needed some extra TLC while the world went mad.

Best served with coconut yogurt, Raspberry Chia Jam (see page 71) and fresh fruit. This is a pretty moist cake, so it's good for toasting.

WHAT YOU'LL NEED

23cm/9in loaf pan

WET INGREDIENTS

3 very ripe bananas (320g/11½oz/
   1¼ cups mashed)
80ml/2¾fl oz/⅓ cup melted coconut oil
80ml/2¾fl oz/⅓ cup oat milk
2 tablespoons maple syrup
½ teaspoon pure vanilla extract

DRY INGREDIENTS

2 tablespoons ground flaxseeds
60g/2¼oz/⅓ cup coconut sugar
60g/2¼oz/⅓ cup rolled oats
½ teaspoon bicarbonate of soda/
   baking soda
1 teaspoon baking powder
1 teaspoon ground cardamom
215g/7½oz/1 cup spelt flour (to make
   gluten free, use buckwheat flour)
pinch of salt

METHOD

Preheat the oven to 200°C/400°F/Gas 6. Grease your loaf pan with a little coconut oil and set aside.

In a bowl, mash the bananas with a fork until they're proper mashed. Add the rest of the wet ingredients and stir until well combined. Add the ground flaxseeds, stir well, then add the rest of the dry ingredients. Mix until well combined, then spoon the mixture into the loaf pan.

Bake for around 35 minutes, or until golden brown and a knife inserted into the middle comes out clean. Turn out of the tin and leave to cool for 10 minutes before serving.

If you don't eat it all in one sitting like me, it will keep for up to 5 days at room temperature (covered).

SQUAT PANCAKES

Serves: 4 (approx. 12 pancakes)   Time: 1 hour 15 minutes

These super-simple pancakes were conjured up when I returned from my jungle life. I had no money and was looking for a job while living in a squat in East London. It was porridge that kept me warm day and night, yet my taste buds craved more. I was jamming with a man at the time who I wanted to impress, but I'm not the kinda girl that would use a nice dress. Instead, I looked in the cupboard to see what I could cook up, and all I had was oats, bananas and milk. So, I blended what I had, and behold, the squat pancake was born.

He loved them and called them "posh pancakes for squat life". I laughed and replied, "Just coz I'm living like this doesn't mean I can't have the best. Life is about balance, bruv."

Stack and serve with coconut yogurt, raspberry chia jam and fresh fruit, and drizzled with maple syrup.

WHAT YOU'LL NEED

Blender
Large non-stick pan

INGREDIENTS

3 medium-ripe bananas
180g/6¼oz/1 cup rolled oats
1 teaspoon ground flaxseeds
375ml/13fl oz/1½ cups oat milk
½ teaspoon coconut oil

FOR THE RASPBERRY CHIA JAM

350g/12¼oz/2¾ cups frozen raspberries
2 tablespoons maple syrup
½ teaspoon of lemon zest
2 tablespoons chia seeds

METHOD

To make the jam, add the raspberries to a saucepan and bring to the boil. Add the maple syrup and lemon zest before turning the heat down and letting it simmer for about 10 minutes. Leave to cool for 5 minutes, then add the chia seeds, stir and leave to set for an hour.

In the meantime, put the bananas, oats and flaxseeds into a blender, then pour in the oat milk bit by bit, blending until you get the consistency of cake batter.

Heat the coconut oil in a large non-stick pan over a medium–low heat. Spoon about 3 tablespoons of the batter per pancake into the pan and cook for a few minutes on both sides until golden brown. Cook the pancakes in batches until all the batter is used up.

Notes...

The Raspberry Chia Jam can be stored in the refrigerator for up to a week.

RUSTIC KIMCHI PANCAKES

Serves: 4   Time: 35 minutes

I fell in love with a woman once, a woman who wanted only savoury things for breakfast. For me, it was sweet that made my heart beat. But I got creating on my boat, and these kimchi pancakes were born. Every time I make them, I am reminded that love has no limits; that love sometimes turns up completely differently to how we expect. And to be open to it and move with it, to not deny what the heart whispers. I always thought I wanted sweet for breakfast; it turns out I like savoury too.

This dish is a blend of savoury spicy kimchi pancakes with a sweet Asian-inspired sauce, earthy mushrooms and earthy greens. It's filling and perfect for brunch, served hot or cold. This dish is to be shared with loved ones, while perhaps reading them a poem of love.

WHAT YOU'LL NEED
Blender
2 non-stick frying pans

INGREDIENTS
140g/5oz/1 cup kimchi
2 spring onions/scallions, finely sliced
    (only use the white part)
1 tablespoon ground flaxseeds
85g/3oz/scant 1 cup chickpea/gram flour
240ml/9fl oz/1 cup water
olive oil
1 punnet of chestnut/cremini mushrooms
    (approx. 200g/7oz), sliced
2 handfuls of spring/collard greens
    or spinach leaves
1 avocado, peeled, pitted and sliced
2 tablespoons sesame seeds
a handful of coriander/cilantro leaves
salt and pepper

FOR THE SAUCE
1 red pepper, deseeded and chopped
    (approx. 200g/7oz/1½ cups chopped)
5 tablespoons light tahini
1 tablespoon tamari
2.5cm/1in piece of root ginger,
    peeled and chopped
1 teaspoon agave syrup
1 garlic clove
1 tablespoon lemon juice
1 red chilli, chopped (optional for
    extra spice)
salt and pepper

METHOD
First, make the pancake batter. Put the kimchi into a bowl and chop with scissors so it's in smaller pieces. Add the spring onions, a pinch of salt and pepper, the ground flaxseeds and chickpea flour, then stir until well combined.

Slowly add the water bit by bit, stirring until you have a thick batter. If it's too thick, add an extra tablespoon of water or kimchi juice. Set aside for 5 minutes while you make the sauce.

Put all the sauce ingredients into the blender and blend together until it's a smooth consistency.

Heat a drizzle of olive oil in a non-stick frying pan over a medium heat, tipping the pan so the oil coats the whole pan. Spoon a big dollop of the batter into the frying pan and squash it down so it's flat and resembles a rustic pancake. Cook for a few minutes on both sides till golden brown. Repeat with the rest of the batter to make 4 pancakes.

Heat a drizzle of olive oil in a separate pan, over a medium heat, then add the mushrooms and cook for 5 minutes (don't stir them too much, as this is what makes them go soggy). Add the spring greens or spinach and sauté gently for a few minutes until lightly cooked.

Divide the pancakes between your plates, top with the greens and mushrooms, add the sliced avocado, drizzle with the sauce and sprinkle with sesame seeds and fresh coriander.

GINGER-INFUSED STRAWBERRY OAT BAKE

Makes: 9 slices   Time: 45 minutes

Inspired by the beloved fruit crumble, these breakfast bars remind me of my childhood. They feel like a dessert, yet they're more nourishing with the chia seeds and almonds. I add a little ground cardamom for a subtle aphrodisiac.

I vary the jammiest of jams with what's in season: strawberries for summer, raspberries and blackberries for autumn and rhubarb for the winter.

WHAT YOU'LL NEED
Saucepan
20cm x 20cm (8in x 8in) baking pan

INGREDIENTS
180g/6¼oz/1 cup rolled oats
180g/6¼oz/1½ cups ground almonds
1 teaspoon ground cardamom
1 teaspoon ground ginger
5 tablespoons agave syrup
120ml/4fl oz/½ cup melted coconut oil

FOR THE STRAWBERRY CHIA JAM
350g/12oz/2 cups ripe strawberries,
    chopped (or you can use frozen)
1 tablespoon agave syrup
1 teaspoon lemon juice
2 drops of geranium essential oil,
    or 1 tablespoon chopped dried
    rose petals (optional)
2 tablespoons chia seeds

METHOD
Preheat the oven to 200°C/400°F/Gas 6 and line the square baking pan with baking parchment.

First, make the jam. Place the strawberries in a saucepan over a medium heat and bring to a simmer. Add the agave syrup, lemon juice and geranium oil, if using, and cook for 10 minutes until the strawberries are soft. You can crush them with a fork as you go.

Once cooked, turn off the heat, add the chia seeds, stir well and set aside.

In a bowl, mix the oats, ground almonds, cardamom and ginger. Add the agave syrup and melted coconut oil and stir well. Spoon three quarters of the oat mix into the lined pan and spread out evenly. Spread over the strawberry jam, then scatter the remaining oat mix over the top. Pop in the oven for 30 minutes until the top starts to golden.

Leave to cool in the tin before cutting into 9 pieces. The bake will last up to 5 days in the refrigerator.

PIMPED UP PORRIGE WITH STEWED APPLES

Serves: 2   Time: 25 minutes

Nana B would tell me how porridge is not only nutritious, it can make us feel rooted, strong and full for a good part of the day. Our ancestors have been surviving on oats for hundreds of years and, being one of the oldest grains on earth, they feel like home.

When apple season hits, I am out and about, a bag in my hand to go scrumping, even in a big city; fusing the ancient with the modern world. Stewing apples with cinnamon is the perfect way to pimp up your porridge.

WHAT YOU'LL NEED
2 saucepans

INGREDIENTS
90g/3¼oz/½ cup porridge oats

375ml/13fl oz/1½ cups oat milk

1 tablespoon coconut sugar

125ml/4fl oz/½ cup water

FOR THE STEWED APPLES
3 apples, cored and cut into cubes
    (approx. 300g/10½oz/2 cups)

2.5cm/1in piece of root ginger, peeled
    and grated

300ml/10½fl oz/1¼ cups water

½ teaspoon ground cinnamon

2 tablespoons coconut sugar (or an
    alternative sweetener of your choice)

TOPPINGS (OPTIONAL)
2 tablespoons coconut yogurt

1 tablespoon maple syrup

a handful of blueberries

a handful of pistachios, chopped

a sprinkle of chopped dried rose petals

METHOD
First, make the stewed apples. Put the apples and ginger into a saucepan over a medium heat. Pour in the water and add the cinnamon and coconut sugar. Bring to a simmer and cook for 15–20 minutes until the apples are soft and most of the water has evaporated. Set aside.

Put the oats and oat milk into a separate saucepan over a medium heat, add the coconut sugar and stir for a few minutes, then add the water and simmer for a few more minutes.

Divide the porridge between your bowls and add a spoonful of stewed apples. If you like, top with the optional toppings. Once cooled, the stewed apples will keep for up to a week in the refrigerator.

FULL MOON GRANOLA

Serves: 10   Time: 35 minutes

They say that on a full moon we should feast and fill our bellies with goodness to give us energy for the next cycle. So this is a time when I make granola, bircher and other pantry delights. I always make time around the full moon to give myself some extra love – and what better way than filling our cupboards with wholesome homemade foods.

Granola is a classic. I have made this all over the world and taught this recipe to so many children. It's great to see young people learning how to make food that is healthy, and that they can have daily. This version has the perfect amount of crunch. I like to keep it pretty simple but you can swap the seeds for nuts if you like. Use it in smoothie bowls, with yoghurt. It's full of fibre and goodness and, best of all, pretty cheap.

WHAT YOU'LL NEED
Baking sheet

DRY INGREDIENTS
250g/8¾oz/3 cups rolled oats
40g/1½oz/⅓ cup sunflower seeds
40g/1½oz/⅓ cup pumpkin seeds
40g/1½oz/⅓ cup flaxseeds
¼ teaspoon ground cardamom
½ teaspoon ground cinnamon
½ teaspoon ground ginger

WET INGREDIENTS
60ml/2fl oz/½ cup maple syrup
120ml/4fl oz/1 cup coconut oil, melted

METHOD
Preheat the oven to 200°C/400°F/ Gas 6. Line a baking sheet with baking parchment.

Mix all the dry ingredients in a large bowl first, stirring until well combined. Then add the wet ingredients and mix, making sure everything is again well combined.

Spread the mixture out on the baking sheet and place in the oven for 20–25 minutes, turning occasionally, until slightly golden.

Remove from the oven and leave to cool before serving, allowing the granola to become more crunchy.

FULL MOON BIRCHER

Serves: 6 Time: 15 minutes + at least 2 hours standing

This Bircher is full of seeds, which contain lots of fibre, protein and potential. Seeds are one of the smallest things in the universe, but they are also one of the most powerful. They represent life and new beginnings. In the right environment, they grow from the dark soil, finding the strength to face the sun. The beautiful thing about seeds is they do not fear light or dark; in fact, they use both to grow. These tiny seeds grow into beautiful plants that give us oxygen and food to feed our loved ones. Without seeds we cannot live, we cannot thrive.

This Bircher is my go-to when I know I am going to be in a rush in the morning. The night before, I mix some Bircher and plant milk in a jar, then the next morning I add a handful of raspberries and run out the door, knowing that when I catch a minute and take a deep breath, I have a breakfast that is gonna nourish deep and taste divine. It's great after a workout too.

This recipe is really versatile, so you can switch up the ingredients according to what you have in your cupboard. Perfect with milk, or on top of smoothie bowls, porridge or yogurt. I like to top mine with fresh fruit.

INGREDIENTS

140g/5oz/¾ cup rolled oats

35g/1¼oz/¼ cup chia seeds

35g/1¼oz/3 tablespoons cacao nibs

85g/3oz/½ cup hemp seeds

70g/2½oz/⅓ cup sunflower seeds

70g/2½oz/scant ½ cup goji berries

70g/2½oz/¾ cup coconut flakes

70g/2½oz/½ cup flaxseeds

1 teaspoon ground cinnamon

1 teaspoon ground ginger

3 tablespoons coconut sugar

TO SERVE

380g/12fl oz/1½ cups of plant milk

chopped fresh fruit, to serve

a sprinkle of chopped dried rose petals,
    to finish

METHOD

In a large jar, mix all the ingredients together well.

Mix a mug of Bircher and a mug and a half of plant milk in a bowl, jar or Tupperware and leave for at least a couple of hours in the refrigerator, preferably overnight, before adding your toppings (I use fresh fruit and dried rose petals) and eating.

Store for up to 3 months in a cool, dry place.

JUICES

When I lived in a raw food community, I learned that fruit was a gift from the gods, that giving yourself fruit was to give yourself life. Fruits beautify and cleanse because they have a high water content, are packed full of vitamins and are charged by the sun's energy. I tell you this: a good juice will bring more vitality into your life.

Humans have a strong natural connection with fruit; as soon as we smell a ripe fruit on the tree we start to salivate. Sipping on a juice is the perfect way to wake up your body in the morning, and juices can also be a refreshing snack throughout the day. They are a great way to get more nutrients into the body.

When I lived in the jungle, we would offer fruit to the trees and rivers daily to say thank you for all of life's bounty.

𝒩otes...
Make sure you chop all your ingredients to the right size for your juicer

All juices serve: 2   Time to make each juice: 15 minutes

CARROT, PINEAPPLE AND MANDARIN JUICE AKA SUNSHINE JUICE

I was dating a man who was a shy guy. He wasn't a man of many words. He was on his journey of trying to find his voice after it had been repressed for years. He would leave the boat at 7am to go to work and, without fail, he would make me a juice and leave it on the side. I learned over time that sometimes you don't need to say I love you; sometimes it's the everyday actions that say it for you.

WHAT YOU'LL NEED
Juicer

INGREDIENTS
1 pineapple, peeled and chopped
2 carrots
3 mandarins, peeled
2.5cm/1in piece of root ginger, peeled

METHOD
Juice all the ingredients and serve over ice if you'd like it chilled.

WATERMELON AND MINT JUICE

I was told by a man named Jerry in the jungle that watermelon is the most nourishing fruit; because it has such a high water content, it can fill the body quickly with nutrients. It's like an infusion of life that will make you smile. Every time I make this juice and sit in the sun, I am reminded of this infusion of life.

WHAT YOU'LL NEED
Juicer

INGREDIENTS
1 watermelon, halved and rind removed
a handful of mint leaves

METHOD
First juice the watermelon and then the mint leaves. Serve over ice if you'd like it chilled.

PINEAPPLE, BEETROOT/ BEETS AND CHILLI JUICE

This juice is a cleanser. A grandmother in the jungle told me that pineapple makes your body fluids taste sweet. So, drink this often and you'll drive your lover crazy. They will lust for more. The secret is out! Side note: drink this the day before. Sweet and spicy.

WHAT YOU'LL NEED
Juicer

INGREDIENTS
1 large pineapple, peeled and chopped
1 beetroot/beet (approx. 220g/8oz), quartered
¼ teaspoon cayenne pepper, plus extra if you like it extra spicy

METHOD
Juice the pineapple and the beetroot, then add the cayenne and stir. Serve over ice if you'd like it chilled, with more cayenne for extra spice, if you like!

APPLE, FENNEL AND BASIL JUICE

Green juice is the most alkalizing thing you can drink. This is inspired by my grandma's apple trees. She tells me it's like a blood infusion from the plants. They give us exactly what we need. It aids digestion and sets the bowels free. When I was having skin and digestive problems, it was green juice that helped me and gave me balance daily.

Fennel is for strength and courage. Ginger assists with that inner creative fire.

WHAT YOU'LL NEED
Juicer

INGREDIENTS
3 apples, cored and chopped
½ bulb of fennel, chopped
2.5cm/1in piece of root ginger, peeled (optional)
1 cucumber, chopped
5 celery stalks, chopped
a handful of basil leaves
a squeeze of lemon

METHOD
Juice all the ingredients and serve over ice if you'd like it chilled.

SMOOTHIE BOWLS

I love a good smoothie bowl. I eat them all year long ... yep, even in winter.

I spent a lot of time in the tropics where there was an abundance of fruit and I had to get creative with it. I love the colours of fruit and I love the way it makes your body feel after you eat it. On retreats, I make smoothie bowls for breakfast or brunch and I see people get so excited about the beauty that is in front of them. I see them connect with nature's beauty through the bright colours and all the toppings. Fruit is the perfect food to give vitality to the body, spirit and mind.

Serves: 2 Time: 10 minutes

MANGO AND BASIL SMOOTHIE BOWL

Sabina, an elder in the jungle, told me that mangoes symbolize fun and play, that we should make time to incorporate that into our daily life. She would leave mangoes outside my door at sunrise, and in return I would create a recipe. We learned from each other. We shared stories of love and pain, and she would regularly laugh at my city ways. She asked why I travelled so far and what was it I was really looking for? I smiled and said, "I wanna learn and explore." She whacked my head with her walking stick and laughed. "Ha, child, everything you are searching for is inside of you. No need to go so far."

WHAT YOU'LL NEED
Blender

INGREDIENTS
3 frozen bananas, chopped
1 large mango, peeled, pitted and chopped
  (you can use frozen)
350ml/12fl oz/1½ cup plant milk (I love oat)
8 basil leaves
1 teaspoon grated root ginger
1 teaspoon spirulina
zest of ½ lime

METHOD
Put all the ingredients into a blender and blend until thick and creamy. If you want a smoothie consistency, you can add 125ml/4fl oz/½ cup more milk.

If your blender is having trouble, add an extra splash of oat milk to give it some help.

Serves: 2   Time: 10 minutes

WILD BLUEBERRY SMOOTHIE BOWL

I heard a story that the wild blueberry plant can be burned but will grow again and return to life. Imagine eating a food that has so much strength that it can resurrect from the dead. A fruit that supports you when you need to rise again.

These little blue fruits are great for the brain and give the liver some love. They taste slightly bitter on their own, but when mixed with banana, they bring an elegant balance and turn this smoothie bowl a colour that you almost can't believe is from nature.

Wild blueberries can be found in the UK on moorlands. They are brighter coloured than the ones you find in the supermarket. I usually buy them frozen, as you won't find these in the city. You can, of course, make this smoothie with regular blueberries.

WHAT YOU'LL NEED
Blender

INGREDIENTS
140g/5oz/1½ cup frozen wild blueberries
350ml/12fl oz/1½ cup oat milk
3 frozen bananas, chopped

METHOD
Put all the ingredients into a blender and blend until thick and creamy.
If you want a smoothie consistency, you can add 125ml/4fl oz/½ cup more milk.

If your blender is having trouble, add an extra splash of oat milk to give it some help.

Optional toppings for each smoothie bowl
* a handful of granola
* an abundance of chopped fruit of your choice
* a drizzle or two of almond or peanut butter
* edible flowers

SMOOTHIES

Over the years, I have got really good at making smoothies. I'll own it, I am a bit of a smoothie snob. Now and then I like to infuse mine with superfoods to enhance my spirit and shift my moods.

Notes...

A great trick I wish I'd known years ago is to use frozen bananas as the base for smoothies, as they create such a creamy texture. The bananas should be very ripe with spots on the skin. It's best to peel and slice them first before freezing. Freezing fruit is a great way to prevent it going to waste and it saves money too. I'm always down the markets getting boxes of bananas that the market vendors are about to get rid of, to make my smoothies even more cost effective. Big up the bananas.

All smoothies serve: 1   Time to make each smoothie: 5 minutes

GOJI, ROSE, COCONUT AND STRAWBERRY SMOOTHIE

Rose is great for the heart and strawberries are for sensuality, blended with goji berries for the perfect boost of vitamin c.

This is a sweet, refreshing smoothie – my go-to when I want to fuel my body and spirit with love. Every time I make it, I remind myself that I can only love someone as deeply as I love myself. Thats why I sprinkle love into everything I do, because I know I can't love you without loving me too.

WHAT YOU'LL NEED
Blender

INGREDIENTS
2 frozen bananas
3 strawberries
1 teaspoon goji berries
2 tablespoons coconut yogurt
250ml/9fl oz/1 cup almond milk
1 teaspoon chopped dried rose petals
1 teaspoon lucuma powder (optional)

METHOD
Put all the ingredients into a blender and blend until smooth.

CACAO SMOOTHIE AKA THE REBEL CHOCOLATE SHAKE

This smoothie is great when you feel a little tired and need a refreshing pick-me-up. It has a rich creamy texture with a slight punch of savoury from the peanuts and salt.

I call this the rebel shake because I was always told as a child that you shouldn't have chocolate for breakfast, or eat lots of cake, and that you only get out the best plates on special occasions. So every time I make this smoothie, I remind myself that I make my own rules and I dance to my own beat. I'll have chocolate for breakfast when I want, and I'll use the best plates every day.

WHAT YOU'LL NEED
Blender

INGREDIENTS
1 tablespoon peanut butter
2 frozen bananas
300ml/10½fl oz/1¼ cups almond milk
2 dates, pitted and chopped
1½ tablespoons cacao powder
1 teaspoon maca powder (optional)
1 teaspoon protein powder (optional)
a pinch of salt

METHOD
Put all the ingredients into a blender and blend until smooth.

PASSION FRUIT AND LIME SMOOTHIE

WHAT YOU'LL NEED
Blender

INGREDIENTS
2 frozen bananas
1 passion fruit, halved and flesh scooped out
1cm/½in piece of root ginger, peeled and chopped
½ teaspoon lime zest
200ml/7fl oz/scant 1 cup almond milk

METHOD
Put all the ingredients into a blender and blend until smooth.

FIG, BANANA AND MINT SMOOTHIE

WHAT YOU'LL NEED
Blender

INGREDIENTS
2 fresh figs, quartered
4 mint leaves
2 frozen bananas
250ml/9fl oz/1 cup oat milk
1 teaspoon maca powder (optional)

METHOD
Put all the ingredients into a blender and blend until smooth.

SALADS AND SOUPS

With every plant feast there will always be a salad. But let me tell you this: no salad should ever be boring. A good salad should make you dance while you eat it. The secret to a banging salad is the dressing and a variety of textures, so get playful and try out your own combinations.

Soups are a history lesson, a reminder of our ancestors and the meals they cooked over fire to create food that warmed the bones and soothed the soul. There are endless possibilities with soups, so here I've provided the ones that nourish me on all the levels.

QUINOA, TOMATO AND AVOCADO SALAD

Serves: 4 as a side   Time: 35 minutes

Every time I make this salad, I think of freedom. When I started my healing journey, my body was detoxing and often felt weak. I was taken to the local witch, and she told my then husband to put onions in my wet socks before wearing them at night to draw out any toxins; to blow the smoke of herbs around my body, to assist unwanted energy in leaving. To eat quinoa, the grain of strength, and avocado to soothe my heart from all the emotions that were to inevitably come from years of suppressing feelings. The plants held me on all the levels. I just had to learn to surrender. And in surrendering came freedom.

This salad is simple, comforting and can give strength. It works well on its own but can complement any dish. I ate this salad every day for months as I was detoxing, not just cause it tasted delicious but I knew I had to start giving my body what it needed: plants that nourish deep.

WHAT YOU'LL NEED
Saucepan

INGREDIENTS
185g/6½oz/1 cup quinoa
500ml/17fl oz/2 cups water
30g/1oz/1 cup basil leaves, torn
200g/7oz/1 cup cherry tomatoes, halved
1 large avocado, peeled, pitted and
    chopped
½ large cucumber, finely chopped
3 tablespoons lemon juice
salt

METHOD
Rinse the quinoa and add to a saucepan with the water and a pinch of salt. Cook over a medium heat for 20 minutes. You'll know when it is ready because the grains pop open. Take off the heat, add the basil, place the lid on the saucepan and leave to steam for 5 minutes.

Once the quinoa has cooled slightly, transfer it to a bowl and stir to separate the grains. Add the tomatoes, avocado and cucumber, then finish with the lemon juice and a pinch of salt.

SPICY LENTILS AND BEETROOT/BEETS SALAD

Serves: 4 as a side   Time: 55 minutes

"Beetroot is the colour of your blood; blood will always connect you to your ancestors; when you connect with your blood, you will remember all who walked before you and all that they fought for, for the life you live now. This is how you remember the power that exists within you."

After years in the jungle, it took some time to settle back in London. For a while, I felt like I didn't fit here or there. Lost between worlds. Yet I would remember my then mother-in-law Elba's wise words as she made beetroot juice. I'm not sure I've ever looked at a beetroot in the same way since.

This salad was created when I had just borrowed enough money for my boat, and I was finally settling down in the land I grew up in. I was exploring the rolling hills and pink skies. I created it in winter when my body craved freshness but needed the earthy, nourishing beetroot to connect me to my ancestors and to keep me warm. This salad is fiery and filling, and packed full of protein.

WHAT YOU'LL NEED

Baking sheet
Frying pan

INGREDIENTS

500g/1lb 2oz beetroots/beets
   (about 6), thinly sliced
olive oil
3 garlic cloves, finely chopped
1 large red chilli, finely chopped (leave
   the seeds in if you want it extra spicy)
1 × 400g/14oz can of green lentils,
   drained and rinsed
a large handful of rocket/arugula
salt and pepper

FOR THE MARINADE

1 tablespoon olive oil
2.5cm/1in piece of root ginger,
   peeled and grated
½ teaspoon agave nectar
1 tablespoon red balsamic vinegar

FOR THE PEANUT DRESSING

2 tablespoons peanut butter
½ teaspoon cayenne pepper
2 teaspoons agave syrup
2 teaspoons tamari
2 teaspoons lemon juice
2 tablespoons water

TO SERVE

2 tablespoons sesame seeds
a handful of chopped chives

METHOD

Preheat the oven to 200°C/400°F/Gas 6.

Arrange the beetroot slices on a baking sheet, sprinkle with salt and drizzle generously with olive oil, making sure they're well covered. Roast in the oven for 45 minutes.

Meanwhile, mix all the marinade ingredients together in a small bowl. Mix all the dressing ingredients together in a separate bowl until well combined. You want a smooth consistency, so if need be, add another tablespoon of water.

Heat a drizzle of olive oil in a frying pan over a medium heat, then add the garlic and chilli and cook for 5 minutes. Add the lentils, season with salt and pepper and fry for 5 minutes.

Once cooled, spoon the lentils onto a large serving plate and spread them out. Place the rocket on top, add a splash of olive oil and lightly toss the leaves. Arrange the roast beetroot on top of the rocket, then spoon over the marinade.

Drizzle the salad with the peanut dressing, then serve sprinkled with sesame seeds and fresh chives.

SPICY MANGO AND PALM HEART SALAD

Serves: 6 as a side   Time: 20 minutes

This salad is simple, sweet and spicy. As with all things, it's about balance. It's so fresh, and it takes me back to when the only trees I would see were palm trees. Palm hearts are packed with protein and mangoes bring the sunshine vibes. It's a dish that will make you want to dance while you eat it.

People often ask me where I buy palm hearts – they're easy to find in most supermarkets with the tinned veg.

INGREDIENTS

1 × 410g/14½oz can of hearts of palm, drained and rinsed

1 large mango (approx. 250g/9oz), peeled, pitted and cut into 1cm/½in cubes

a small handful of coriander/cilantro leaves, chopped

2 spring onions/scallions, sliced

1 avocado, peeled, pitted and cut into small cubes

¼ teaspoon ground cumin

¼ teaspoon dried chilli/hot pepper flakes

3 tablespoons lime juice

salt and pepper

2 tablespoons Sweet and Super Spicy Coconut Pepitas (see page 173) (optional)

METHOD

Cut the palm hearts in half and then into 1cm/½in slices.

Place in a bowl, add the mango and the chopped coriander, then gently mix. Add the spring onions and the avocado, then gently mix again.

Season with a pinch of salt and pepper, then sprinkle over the cumin and chilli flakes. Squeeze over the lime juice and stir.

Serve scattered with pepitas, if desired.

One evening at one of my ceremonial supper clubs, we were feasting on plants, dishing up the plates, sharing stories and ponderings.

Someone asked me, "Is this your purpose, Frankie?"

I replied, "I hate this question. I feel we get so lost in it on this side of the world."

A woman called Dee piped up. "My family says we don't talk of death enough. If we thought and spoke about death more like we do in my birth country, India, purpose wouldn't be such a thing."

A man who had a strong Welsh accent replied, "I have been stuck in my life so much figuring out my purpose, worrying I will never find it. Asking myself often, what is my calling in life?"

A lady called Tish replied, "Well, maybe if we spoke about death more, maybe we would see the things we will regret, and we would focus on those instead."

The Welsh guy replied, "Yeah, I guess if I'm on my deathbed, I won't be saying I wish I'd found my purpose!"

"Yeah," I replied, "now, you'll be saying: I wish I had lived more and felt all the emotions. Well, that's my purpose, to live and to feel. I was born a human and my purpose is to experience all the human emotions and feelings!"

We then made a toast. "Fuck purpose! Here's to celebrating being human and all the madness it brings."

It's beautiful to see strangers connect so deeply and open up so freely.

SIMPLE GARDEN SALAD

Serves: 4 as a side   Time: 15 minutes

I believe we all need a quick salad recipe that will elevate garden greens and complement any plant feast. A no-faff salad that gives you what you need. The dressing has a slight kick to it, while harnessing sweet energy; make sure you add a good lashing to the salad. You can use any salad greens for this recipe.

INGREDIENTS

150g/5½oz mixed salad leaves/greens

15g/½oz/½ cup flat leaf parsley leaves, chopped

½ cucumber, cut into matchsticks

6 small tomatoes, cut into quarters (approx. 180g/6¼oz/1½ cups)

2 spring onions/scallions, sliced

1 avocado, peeled, pitted and chopped

2 tablespoons Walnut and Fennel Seed Dukkah (see page 171), to serve

FOR THE DRESSING

5 tablespoons olive oil

1 tablespoon wholegrain mustard

1 tablespoon agave syrup

1 tablespoon lemon juice

a pinch of cayenne pepper (or more if you like spice)

salt and pepper

METHOD

Put the salad leaves into a salad bowl, then add the parsley leaves, cucumber, tomatoes, spring onions and avocado.

In a small bowl, mix all the dressing ingredients together well, season, then pour over the salad and toss.

Serve sprinkled with walnut dukkah.

KOHLRABI AND APPLE SALAD

Serves: 4 as a side   Time: 15 minutes

I never really understood kohlrabi; I tried it so many times but I just couldn't find my flow with it, and on a level I didn't really like it. Then one day it all changed. A friend made me a salad with kohlrabi, apple and tarragon – the flavours together blew my mind. It's funny how someone can make you something and just like that your whole perspective can change.

I went back to my boat, got witchy and started creating, added a sauce and a sprinkle of bits and it went to a whole other level. This creations is a fresh dish with crunch, perfect for summer and to compliment a BBQ or hearty plant feast.

WHAT YOU'LL NEED
Mandolin (or you can use a grater)
Blender

INGREDIENTS
2 small kohlrabi (approx. 400g/14oz), peeled
2 large Braeburn apples, cored
4 tablespoons light tahini
2 tablespoons chopped chives
8 tablespoons water
2 tablespoons lemon juice
1 teaspoon garlic granules
1 teaspoon chopped tarragon leaves
olive oil
salt and pepper

TO SERVE
2 tablespoons Hemp Seed and Sesame Dukkah (see page 170)
edible flowers

METHOD
Slice the kohlrabi and the apples using a mandolin and then cut into matchsticks (you can do this without a mandolin but it will take longer, or alternatively you can use a grater).

In a blender, blend the tahini, chives, water, lemon juice, garlic granules and a large pinch of salt and pepper until smooth; if it's too thick, add a little more water. Spoon the sauce onto a large plate.

Add the chopped tarragon to the apple and kohlrabi, drizzle with olive oil, mix well, then stack on top of the sauce.

Serve sprinkled with the dukkah and some colourful flowers.

INSPIRED BY SPRING SALAD

Serves: 4 as a side   Time: 45 minutes

Courgette ribbons drenched with wild garlic pesto, with asparagus and three-cornered leeks on a bed of baked butternut squash and mixed leaves. This salad is all things spring. My grandma tells me that when the earth awakens after winter, the first of the plants that grow are bitter, because the earth always give us what we need. Wild garlic, three-cornered leeks and asparagus help to detox our bodies after an indulgent winter. The butternut balances the bitterness with its sweetness and gives some grounding energy.

You can make the pesto without the wild garlic, simply replacing with extra parsely, and if it's not the season for three-cornered leeks, then opt for spring onions instead.

WHAT YOU'LL NEED

Vegetable peeler

Roasting pan

Food processor

INGREDIENTS

1 butternut squash, peeled, deseeded
   and cut into cubes

olive oil

1 bunch of asparagus (approx. 200g/7oz),
   woody ends removed, cut into
   2.5cm/1in pieces

2 courgettes/zucchini, peeled into ribbons

100g/3½oz mixed salad leaves/greens

2 three-cornered leeks, finely chopped,
   plus their flowers to garnish

1 ripe pear, cored and sliced

salt and pepper

FOR THE WILD GARLIC PESTO

30g/1oz/1 cup wild garlic leaves

40g/1½oz/1 cup parsley leaves

40g/1½oz/1 cup basil leaves

2 tablespoons lemon juice

130g/4¾oz/scant 1 cup cashews

7 tablespoons water

6 tablespoons olive oil

1 tablespoon nutritional yeast

a large pinch of salt

FOR THE DRESSING

2 tablespoons olive oil

1 teaspoon lemon juice

1 teaspoon agave syrup

a large pinch of cayenne pepper

a pinch of salt

METHOD

Preheat the oven to 200°C/400°F/Gas 6.

Arrange the butternut squash cubes in a roasting pan, drizzle with olive oil and sprinkle with a good pinch of salt. Bake for 35 minutes until soft but still with some bite.

Meanwhile, blend all the ingredients for the pesto in a food processor until well combined. You may need to scrape down the sides a few times so everything is incorporated. (The pesto will last for up to a week in the refrigerator.)

Add the asparagus to the roasting pan with the squash for the final 15 minutes, adding a little extra olive oil if needed. You want it to still have some bite too. Allow to cool slightly.

Meanwhile, toss the courgette ribbons with 4 tablespoons of the pesto so they're well covered. Mix all the dressing ingredients in a small bowl until well combined.

Put the salad leaves, chopped three-cornered leeks, and roasted asparagus and butternut squash into a serving bowl. Pour over the dressing and mix well. Place the pesto-drenched courgette ribbons on top with the pear slices. Season to taste, then garnish with the three-cornered leek flowers and serve.

GREEN VIBES SOUP

Serves: 4 Time: 45 minutes

Green just makes us feel better, it's a colour that represents nature. This soup was created when the cold had hit hard on the boat. My body was craving something deeply nourishing. My grandma called and told me, "Don't forget green is the colour connected to the heart."

WHAT YOU'LL NEED
Large non-stick pan
Blender/hand-held/immersion blender

INGREDIENTS
1 tablespoon olive oil
2 garlic cloves, crushed
3 potatoes, cut into small cubes (approx. 450g/1lb/3 cups cubed potatoes)
2 leeks, sliced (approx. 250g/9oz/2 cups sliced leeks)
300g/10½oz broccoli, broken into florets
700ml/24fl oz/3 cups water
240ml/9fl oz/1 cup oat milk
1 tablespoon nutritional yeast
150g/5½oz/1 cup peas (frozen work too)
1 tablespoon vegan bouillon powder
a handful of flat leaf parsley leaves
juice of ½ lemon
¼ teaspoon dried chilli/hot pepper flakes
salt and pepper
a handful of Sweet and Super-Spicy Coconut Pepitas (see page 173), to serve

FOR THE LEMON TAHINI CREAM
3 tablespoons of light tahini
4 tablepsoons of water
1 tablepsoon of lemon juice
large pinch of salt
1/4 teaspoon of agave

METHOD
Heat the olive oil in a pan over a medium heat and add the garlic, potatoes, leeks, broccoli and a large pinch of salt. Cook for 5 minutes until the veg starts to sweat and soften.

Pour in the water and the oat milk, add the nutritional yeast, peas, bouillon, ¾ of the parsley leaves and a large pinch of pepper. Cook for 25 minutes until the veg has softened.

Add the lemon juice and chilli flakes, then transfer the soup to a blender and blitz until smooth. You can also use a hand blender if you have one of them knocking about.

To prepare the garnishes, chop the remaining parsley leaves. Add the lemon tahini cream ingredients to a small bowl and use a fork to whisk until well combined and of a smooth consistency.

Serve the soup with an extra pinch of pepper, sprinkled with pepitas and a drizzle of the lemon tahini cream, and scattered with the chopped parsley.

CHUNKY ROOT SOUP

Serves: 2–3 Time: 55 minutes

When I feel overwhelmed and my mind is living in the future, or when the sadness arises and I feel disconnected from the world, I remember it is in these moments I should connect with the Earth. "Let her ground you, let her hold you." As you eat foods that are grown under the earth, their rooted energy can flow through you and bring comfort and ease. From the roots we rise.

The vegetables in this soup are all grown under the earth. It has assisted in bringing more balance after breakups, comforted clients after plant ceremony retreats and nurtured after festivals. It can give comfort when you feel like you need a little TLC.

I've put nettles in too, as they are full of iron and easy to find, so they're a really good way to get you foraging in nature. Foraging for nettle leaves can really help soothe the mind. The soup tastes delicious without them, but they add extra nutrients and a pinch more of that earthy vibe.

WHAT YOU'LL NEED
Large non-stick pan

INGREDIENTS
1 tablespoon olive oil

1 onion, chopped

3 garlic cloves, finely chopped

2 carrots, chopped

5 potatoes, cut into cubes

2 leeks, sliced

1 tablespoon thyme leaves

1 tablespoon oregano leaves (you can use
  dried oregano if you haven't got fresh)

1 chilli, chopped

900ml/31fl oz/3¾ cups water

1 vegetable stock cube

1 teaspoon ground cumin

1 tablespoon nutritional yeast

1 tablespoon lemon juice

a large handful of nettle leaves (optional)

salt and pepper

METHOD
Heat the olive oil in a pan over a medium heat, then add the onion and garlic. Cook for a couple of minutes until the onion has slightly softened. Add the carrots, potatoes, leeks, thyme, oregano and chilli. Cook for 5 minutes to really get them herbs infused.

Pour in the water and crumble in the stock cube. Add the cumin, nutritional yeast and lemon juice. Season with a pinch of salt and pepper, then add the nettle leaves, if using. Cook for 35 minutes until everything has softened, then serve.

BUTTERNUT SOUP

Serves: 2   Time: 55 minutes

This soup was created when I lived in a house with no roof in between the sea and the desert; a time when I learned to truly trust the universe. We would write lyrics to songs on the walls so I could improve my Spanish. We would sing to the Earth, make art and smoke a lot of weed. It was a house full of people that had left their homes in hope of a better life, a simple life of trust and connection.

In the day, my then husband and I would sell jewellery on the streets. We had little money, but I would cook this beautiful soup for the whole community. We'd swap stories of culture and philosophy.

It's a warming soup that's simple and cheap and has the colour of the sun. They say the colour orange can help fuel creativity. Perfect with quinoa, plantain (see page 156), guacamole and pico de gallo (see page 116) and padrón peppers (see page 134).

WHAT YOU'LL NEED

Large non-stick pan
Blender/hand-held/immersion blender

INGREDIENTS

1½ tablespoons coconut oil
1 white onion, sliced
2 garlic cloves, finely chopped
2.5cm/1in piece of root ginger, peeled and
    finely chopped
1 tablespoon chopped rosemary leaves,
    plus extra to serve
2 carrots, chopped
1 large butternut squash, peeled, deseeded
    and chopped (approx. 1kg/2lb 4oz)
    (you can use frozen if you want)
700ml/24fl oz/3 cups water
1 vegetable stock cube
½ tablespoon lemon juice
salt and pepper

TO SERVE

a handful of unsweetened desiccated/dried
    shredded coconut
a handful of Sweet and Super-Spicy
    Coconut Pepitas (see page 173)

METHOD

Heat the coconut oil in a pan over a medium heat and add the onion, garlic and ginger. Stir for a minute or so, then add the chopped rosemary, carrots and butternut squash. Cook for 10 minutes until the veggies start to soften slightly. Keep stirring so they don't stick to the pan.

Pour in the water and crumble in the stock cube. Cook for around 35 minutes until the butternut is very soft. Add the lemon juice.

If you like your soup smooth, carefully transfer the soup to a blender or use a hand blender and blitz until smooth. Season with salt and pepper.

Pour into bowls and serve sprinkled with fresh rosemary, black pepper, desiccated coconut and pepitas.

BIG PLATES

The hearty ones. The main events. I like to serve one of these with a few small plates to create a plant feast, or sometimes I will just serve one on its own, perhaps with a salad, just for me. I give options if you want them as a main or if you want to serve them as part of a feast. They all work and flow together. There are no rules on how to make your own plant feast, just give it a go and create. I hope these plates give you as much joy as they have my community and me.

LOADED SWEET POTATO WEDGES WITH ALL THE PLANT THRILLS

Serves: 4 as a side or 2 as a main   Time: 50 minutes + 4–6 hours soaking

This dish is comforting, filling and nourishing. All the Latin flavours, drenched with cashew cream. The pico de gallo brings the freshness, and the frijoles give the kick.

I was told that the sweet potato is a vegetable that roots and grounds you; the one that brings peace. It grows under the earth in the dark, yet it has the colour of the sun. A reminder that even in the darkest of places, sunshine still comes.

This dish was created when my then husband finally got his visa accepted in the UK. He lived here for 5 years and it was wild seeing the city through his eyes. To be honest, it was a real shock for him after living and travelling his whole life in South America. He loved the diversity of the people but found the rules hard; he would say that even the grass is controlled here. He couldn't understand how people walked past each other and wouldn't say hello or even look each other in the eyes. He would say, "Everyone is on their phone and looking at the ground. Do they forget that there is a sky and trees?" It made me see London a little differently too.

While we lived in our little single-bed bedsit in Hackney, I would create lots of Latin-inspired dishes to remind him of home. That's the thing about spices and dishes from where you're from, they can take you right back to a place of comfort, even when the world outside feels chaotic. No matter how chaotic my ife feels, I guess my journey has always been to find peace within the chaos. This dish is that. It's a dish inspired by two worlds meeting in love and trying to find their way.

Perfect with rice, plantain (see page 156), Padrón peppers (see page 135) and Spicy Mango and Palm Heart Salad (see page 98).

WHAT YOU'LL NEED

Roasting pan

Blender

Frying pan

Squeezy bottle (optional)

INGREDIENTS

4 sweet potatoes, washed and cut
    into wedges

olive oil

salt and pepper

FOR THE CASHEW CREAM

70g/2½oz/½ cup raw cashews, soaked
    for 4–6 hourss, then drained

1 tablespoon nutritional yeast

2 tablespoons lemon juice

½ teaspoon apple cider vinegar

120ml/4fl oz/½ cup water

a big pinch of salt

FOR THE SPICY BEAN FRIJOLES

olive oil

1 garlic clove, chopped

½ teaspoon paprika

½ teaspoon ground cumin

a pinch of cayenne pepper (or more if you
    like spice)

1 × 400g/14oz can of pinto beans, drained
    and rinsed

1 × 400g/14oz can of chopped tomatoes

a handful of coriander/cilantro leaves,
    chopped, plus extra to garnish

salt and pepper

FOR THE PICO DE GALLO

250g/9oz tomatoes, deseeded,
    then finely chopped

1 small red onion, finely chopped

a handful of coriander/cilantro leaves,
    chopped

1 tablespoon lemon juice

a big pinch of salt

FOR THE GUACAMOLE

2 avocados, peeled, pitted and chopped

1 tablespoon lemon juice

a big pinch of salt

METHOD

Preheat the oven to 200°C/400°F/Gas 6.

Arrange the sweet potato wedges in a
roasting pan, add a good drizzle of olive
oil and a good pinch of salt and pepper.
Roast for around 40 minutes until soft,
turning them over halfway through.

Meanwhile, to make the cashew cream,
blitz all the ingredients in a blender
until smooth (you want the consistency
of sour cream). Add an extra tablespoon
or so of water if it's too thick or your
blender needs a little help. It will keep in
the refrigerator for up to a week.

For the spicy bean frijoles, heat a
splash of olive oil in a frying pan over a
medium heat, add the garlic and fry for
a couple of minutes. Add the paprika,
cumin, cayenne, pinto beans, canned
tomatoes and a pinch of salt and pepper.

Leave to simmer for 15 minutes, stirring occasionally. Add the fresh chopped coriander leaves.

For the pico de gallo, gently mix all the ingredients together in a serving bowl until well combined.

For the guacamole, put the ingredients into a separate bowl and mash with a fork. You want it well combined but not completely smooth.

To assemble, arrange the sweet potatoes on a large serving plate. Spoon the spicy beans on top, then the guacamole and then the pico de gallo. Drizzle over the cashew creme (you can use a squeezy bottle for this, if you have one) and finally garnish with extra chopped coriander.

AUBERGINE/EGGPLANT, CHICKPEA PANCAKES AND SPICY MANGO CHUTNEY

Serves: 4 as a main   Time: 1¼ hours

The balance of flavours in this dish hits all the spots. My mum first made me a jar of spicy mango chutney inspired by her friend Kish. Back on my boat, I created chickpea pancakes with creamy aubergine/eggplant, looked in my refrigerator, saw the chutney and thought, "I'll see how this goes." To my surprise it tasted heavenly. The chutney took the dish to the next level.

You can make the pancakes in advance and reheat before serving. When I'm on a retreat, I make them the day before, so I have more time to make other plant delights or to just have more moments to chill.

The spicy mango chutney is kind of in between a chutney and a sauce. Sweet and spicy. I always like to go down the market and see if there is a box of overripe mangoes that are going cheap, then I'll make a big batch of this stuff and smother it on everything. I'll gift it to friends and family. I even have it with porridge in the mornings. It keeps in an airtight container in the refrigerator for up to a month.

WHAT YOU'LL NEED

Roasting pan
Saucepan
2 small frying pans

INGREDIENTS

3 aubergines/eggplants, cut into small cubes
    (approx. 700g/1lb 9oz/7 cups chopped)
olive oil
1 tablespoon mustard seeds
1 teaspoon ground cumin
2 garlic cloves, finely chopped
½ teaspoon dried chilli/hot pepper flakes
¼ teaspoon ground coriander

1 teaspoon garam masala
200g/7oz/¾ cup coconut yogurt
2 tablespoons lemon juice
30g/1oz/1 cup coriander/cilantro
    leaves, chopped
salt and pepper

FOR THE SPICY MANGO CHUTNEY

1 tablespoon olive oil
1 tablespoon grated root ginger
1 tablespoon cumin seeds
¼ teaspoon ground cinnamon
½ teaspoon dried chilli/hot pepper flakes
½ teaspoon ground fenugreek
1 teaspoon nigella seeds

4 ripe mangoes, chopped (approx.
  1.8kg/4lb/6 cups fresh mango, or
you can use defrosted frozen mango)
4 tablespoons agave syrup
¼ teaspoon salt
a pinch of black pepper

FOR THE CHICKPEA PANCAKES
180g/6¼oz/1½ cups chickpea/gram flour
1 teaspoon ground cumin
¼ teaspoon salt
1 tablespoon flaxseeds
450ml/15½fl oz/1¾ cups warm water
olive oil

TO SERVE
a handful of rocket/arugula
chopped spring onions/scallions
edible flowers

METHOD
Preheat the oven to 220°C/425°F/Gas 7.

Arrange the aubergine on a roasting pan, sprinkle with salt and leave for a few minutes to draw out the bitterness. Add a glug of olive oil and mix until coated. Roast for 40 minutes, turning them halfway, until they are soft.

Meanwhile, make the chutney. Heat the olive oil in a saucepan over a low heat, then add the ginger and cumin seeds. Cook for a few minutes before adding the rest of the spices, the mango, agave, salt and pepper. Cook for about 15 minutes until it becomes a bit mushy.

Heat a drizzle of olive oil in a frying pan over a medium heat, then add the mustard seeds. Fry for a minute, then add the cumin, garlic, chilli flakes, ground coriander and garam masala. Once the mustard seeds start to pop, transfer the contents of the pan to a bowl, then add the yogurt, lemon juice and some salt and pepper. Stir well, then fold in the fresh coriander. Set aside.

To make the pancakes, mix the dry ingredients in a bowl, then add 240ml/9fl oz/1 cup of the water and whisk until there are no lumps. Slowly add the rest of the water, whisking continuously, until a batter forms. If the mixture thickens too much, add an extra tablespoon of water to loosen.

Place a small frying pan over a low heat and add a drizzle of olive oil, covering the bottom of the pan. Add 3 tablespoons of the batter and cook for a few minutes on both sides until golden. If it doesn't flip easy, it may need a little longer. Repeat with the remaining batter to make 8 pancakes in total.

Add the cooked aubergine to the yogurt and mix well. Serve the pancakes with a couple of spoonfuls of the aubergine on top and a dollop of the mango chutney. Top with a handful of rocket, sprinkle over some chopped spring onions and finish with a few edible flowers!

BALANCED ROOTS

Serves: 4 as a main   Time: 1 hour + 4–6 hours soaking

This recipe is inspired by the UK, the land that I call home, and my time spent in the jungle. It took me a while to see that I was surrounded by nature. I used to think everything I needed was outside of myself. Until I started looking right where I was. That's when I began to see beauty all around me, even in London, and to feel more content.

When living on a boat, you can't not be connected to the seasons. This dish reminds me of autumn, and balance is what I think of when making it: raw cashew cream and raw pesto, curly kale full of nutrients, grounding butternut squash and shiitake mushrooms.

This is the dish I created for Jamie's Cookbook Challenge. It takes longer than others and is ideally served as part of a plant feast with various small plates. It is the perfect way to slow down and come home to yourself.

WHAT YOU'LL NEED

Roasting pan

Blender

Food processor

Large non-stick pan

INGREDIENTS

2 butternut squash (approx. 800g/28oz
    each), peeled, deseeded and cut into
    1cm/½in moons

olive oil

250g/9oz curly kale, tough stalks removed

1 garlic clove, roughly chopped

1 punnet of mushrooms (I like to use
    shiitake), roughly sliced (approx.
    150g/5¼oz/1½ cups)

2 avocados, peeled, pitted and sliced

8 cherry tomatoes, quartered

salt and pepper

FOR THE CASHEW CREAM

140g/5oz/1 cup raw cashews soaked
    for 4–6 hours, then drained

250ml/9fl oz/1 cup water

1 teaspoon smoked garlic granules

1 teaspoon black peppercorns

3 tablespoons lemon juice

¼ teaspoon salt

1 tablespoon nutritional yeast

FOR THE WILD NETTLE PESTO

30g/1oz/1 cup nettle leaves

60g/2¼oz/2 cups basil leaves

40g/1½oz/¼ cup hulled hemp seeds

2 teaspoons lemon juice

a pinch of salt

125ml/4fl oz/½ cup olive oil

TO GARNISH

a handful of pistachios, crushed

1 chilli, chopped

amaranth micro herbs and edible flowers

METHOD

Preheat the oven to 220°C/425°F/Gas 7.

Arrange the butternut squash in a roasting pan, drizzle with olive oil, add a good pinch of salt and mix until the squash is coated. Roast for 35 minutes until softened but still with a bit of bite.

While the butternut squash is cooking, make the other elements of the dish. To make the cashew cream, blitz all the ingredients in a blender, adding the water bit by bit, until smooth (you want the consistency of sour cream). Transfer to a bowl and set aside.

To make the nettle pesto, blanch the nettle leaves in boiling water for 2 minutes, then drain, rinse with cold water and squeeze to extract as much water as possible. Blitz all the pesto ingredients in a food processor, adding the oil bit by bit, until combined but still chunky. Transfer to a bowl and set aside.

Break up the kale a little, then pulse in the blender until broken down further and the colour turns a darker green. Add a pinch of salt.

Heat a splash of olive oil in a pan over a low heat, then add the garlic and the mushrooms. Cook for about 10 minutes until the mushrooms have softened, then turn the heat off, add the kale and stir. The heat in the pan will soften the kale a little more. Season to taste.

To assemble, arrange the butternut squash on a serving plate. Spoon the pesto on top. Drizzle with half the cashew cream. Add the kale and mushrooms and drizzle with the remaining cashew cream. Arrange the avocado slices and tomatoes on top, then garnish with the crushed pistachios, chilli and micro herbs and flowers, if using.

NOURISHING GRAINS

Serves: 4 as a main   Time: 35 minutes

A long time ago, a grandmother in the jungle told me that quinoa has a universe inside it. That it was the mother grain, full of protein and strength. No one had spoken to me about food like that before, or told me a story about a single grain. To see such beauty in a single grain. To see such beauty in food. She told me, "If you eat food from the earth, you will feel connected to her, and in return connect to yourself." It was during this very conversation that I learned that food wasn't about numbing; it was about nourishing and connecting.

This recipe is a fusion of a Latin grain with an Asian-inspired sauce, a retreat classic. I love the freshness of the nourishing green sauce, which can be used as a salad dressing too. If you want to make it into a raw dish, which is perfect for summer, keep the peppers, carrots and courgettes raw and leave out the quinoa. I add the quinoa in colder months.

WHAT YOU'LL NEED

Juliennne peeler (optional)

Spiralizer or mandolin (optional)

Saucepan

Frying pan

Blender

INGREDIENTS

360g/12½oz/2 cups quinoa

1l/35fl oz/4¼ cups water

30g/1oz/¾ cups coriander/cilantro leaves, chopped

2 tablespoons lemon juice

1 tablespoon coconut oil

2 red peppers, deseeded and sliced

6 carrots, julienned (either using a juliennne peeler or knife)

2 courgettes/zucchini, spiralized (I use the smallest setting on my spiralizer) or thinly sliced lengthways (either using a mandolin or knife)

salt

4 lime wedges, to serve

FOR THE GREEN SAUCE

250g/9oz/1 cup almond butter

1 tablespoon tamari

2 tablespoons grated root ginger

1 chilli (or use less if you're not into spice)

1 garlic clove, peeled

3 tablespoons lemon juice

1 tablespoon lime juice

300ml/10½fl oz/1¼ cups water

60g/2¼oz/1½ cups basil leaves

25g/1oz/scant 1 cup coriander/cilantro leaves

2 tablespoons agave syrup

a pinch of salt

TO GARNISH

a handful of crushed peanuts or chopped Tamari Spiced Almonds (see page 172)

1 tablespoon black sesame seeds

edible flowers

METHOD

Put the quinoa, water and a pinch of salt into a saucepan over a medium-low heat. Cook for 15–20 minutes until all the water has been absorbed, then turn off the heat and put the lid on to allow the quinoa to steam for 5 minutes. Add the chopped coriander leaves, lemon juice and some salt to taste. Set aside.

Heat the coconut oil in a frying pan over a low heat, then add the red peppers, carrots and courgettes. Cook for roughly 7 minutes until the veggies soften but still have a bit of crunch. Add salt to taste.

Meanwhile, to make the green sauce, blitz all the ingredients in a blender until well combined. Pour half the sauce over the lightly cooked veggie noodles and stir until coated.

To assemble, divide the remaining sauce between 4 pasta bowls. Spoon 3 heaped tablespoons of the quinoa on top of the sauce in each bowl. Top with the vegetable noodles, then garnish with the peanuts or almonds, sesame seeds and edible flowers. Serve each bowl with a wedge of lime for squeezing over.

SPICY CREAMED JERK SHROOMS WITH WILD RICE

Serves: 4 as a side or 2 as a main   Time: 45 minutes

We all have friends who are more like family, chosen family. They have that feeling of home and comfort. Not connected by blood but connected by soul.

I was living in a damp squat that had mould all over it. I didn't care; it was home for me. I had my own space and I was happy. My friend Subrina came to visit. "Frankie, you can't live here." She gave me her keys and insisted I slept on her sofa. I was there for 5 months while I made enough money for a deposit for a bedsit. Subrina would cook the most amazing dishes, full of flavour and with the perfect amount of spice. Jerk chicken was her speciality. We would share the sides that were just plants. I would sit on the kitchen step and watch her cook. We would swap tips and talk of all the things we could create with jerk spice.

She would tell me stories of her Jamaican grandma and I would tell her stories of my Nana B. She would be like, "Baby girl, you need more herbs and spice in dem dishes." So, I created this. It reminds me of home. We think of home as a place but sometimes it can be people. People with an open heart and a good soul. This meal takes me right back to this scene, a place of comfort, a place of safety and a home with no mould.

This dish is quick, comforting and spicy. A fusion of worlds and heritages. I like to serve this with a side of plantain (see page 156), avocado and simple greens (see page 151).

WHAT YOU'LL NEED
Frying pan
Saucepan

INGREDIENTS
olive oil
1 white onion, sliced
1 garlic clove, finely chopped
2 red peppers, deseeded and sliced into strips
1 tablespoon jerk seasoning

2 tablespoons chopped thyme leaves, plus 1 sprig to garnish
1 punnet of chestnut/cremini mushrooms (approx. 250g/9oz), sliced
200g/7oz/ cup cherry tomatoes, halved
125ml/4fl oz/½ cup oat cream
1 tablespoon tomato purée/paste
180g/6¼oz/1 cup white rice
1 chilli, chopped (if you want it extra hot)
salt

METHOD

Heat a good glug of olive oil in a frying pan over a medium heat and add the onion, garlic and red peppers. Fry for 10 minutes until the peppers start to soften. Add the jerk seasoning and thyme, stir for a minute or so, then add the mushrooms and cherry tomatoes and fry for 5 minutes. Add the oat cream and tomato purée. Add a pinch of salt, then cook for 20 minutes.

Meanwhile, cook the rice in a saucepan of salted boiling water according to the package directions.

Spoon the rice into a serving bowl, then layer the shrooms on top to create height. Add a fresh thyme sprig on top for garnish.

BUTTER BEAN AND SWEET PAPAS COCONUT STEW

Serves: 4 as a side or 2 as a main   Time: 55 minutes

Fire on, tunes pumping, I created this dish that nourishes and comforts using left-over bits in my refrigerator. Working with what you've got is an invitation to get experimental, to get playful. Take time to learn each herb and seasoning.

My tips for creating a new dish: choose a few vegetables, fry some garlic and onion, and season. Add your veg. Work out if you want a creamy dish. I often add coconut yogurt or milk balanced with fresh tomatoes. Or sometimes I flow with dry. Finish with salt and pepper and a sprinkle of herbs – and behold a dish is born.

Serve with a side of avocado, rice and boujie broccoli (see page 148).

WHAT YOU'LL NEED
Saucepan

INGREDIENTS
1 tablespoon coconut oil

1 onion, finely chopped

2 garlic cloves, finely chopped

1 small green chilli, finely chopped

1 teaspoon grated root ginger

1 tablespoon cumin seeds

4 sweet potatoes (approx. 800g/1lb 12oz), peeled and cut into small chunks

2 carrots, finely chopped

1 red pepper, peeled, deseeded and chopped

700ml/24fl oz/3 cups water

a large handful of spinach leaves

1 × 400g/14oz can of butter/lima beans, drained

juice of 1 lemon

a handful of coriander/cilantro leaves, chopped

3 tablespoons coconut yogurt

salt and pepper

Sweet and Super-Spicy Coconut Pepitas (see page 173), to serve

METHOD
Heat the coconut oil in a saucepan over a medium heat, then add the onion, garlic, chilli, ginger and cumin seeds. Cook for a few minutes until the onion has softened.

Add the sweet potatoes, carrots and red pepper and cook for about 10 minutes, stirring constantly so they don't stick to the bottom of the pan. Add the water and the spinach, season with salt and pepper and cook for 25 minutes until the vegetables are lovely and soft.

Add the butter beans and coconut yogurt to the stew and stir well. Cook for 5 more minutes before squeezing in the lemon juice and adding the chopped coriander. Garnish with a small drizzle of coconut yogurt, pepitas and flowers.

CHIMICHURRI CAULIFLOWER LOADED WITH PICO DE GALLO

Serves: 4 as a side or 2 as a main   Time: 50 minutes

When I first started eating more plants many moons ago, vegan food was pretty bland and pretty basic. I remember going for dinner and eating a roasted cauliflower and thinking WTF is this. It was so dry, with no sauce, expensive and it didn't fill me up. It did however get me thinking about how I can make it better and as healthy and delicious as possible. That's the thing about not liking something, or there being a lack of options: it can be an invitation to get in the kitchen and make it better. This is how new creations are born.

This roasted cauliflower is smothered with a tart chimichurri sauce, loaded with sweet tomatoes, and sprinkled with spicy, crunchy pepitas. It's all about the layers! Serve with plantain (see page 156), Cumin and Garlic Potatoes (see page 146), Quinoa, Tomato and Avocado Salad (see page 95), and Spicy Mango and Palm Heart Salad (see page 98) for an epic feast.

WHAT YOU'LL NEED
Baking sheet
Food processor

INGREDIENTS
1 large cauliflower (or 2 small), cut
  lengthways into 2cm/¾in slices
3 tablespoons olive oil
½ teaspoon ground cumin
salt and pepper
a handful of Sweet and Super-Spicy
  Coconut Pepitas (see page 173), to serve

FOR THE CHIMICHURRI
15g/½oz/½ cup mint leaves
40g/1½oz/1 cup flat leaf parsley leaves

40g/1½oz/1 cup coriander/cilantro leaves
juice of 1 lemon
3 jalapeños, deseeded
4 teaspoons ground cumin
1 garlic clove, peeled
¼ teaspoon dried chilli/hot pepper flakes
olive oil
a large pinch of salt and pepper

FOR THE PICO DE GALLO
5 large tomatoes (I use Roma, approx.
  450g/1lb), deseeded and finely chopped
1 small red onion, finely chopped
a handful of coriander/cilantro leaves,
  chopped
2 tablespoons lemon juice
a pinch of salt

METHOD

Preheat the oven to 200°C/400°F/Gas 6.

Arrange the cauliflower slices on a baking sheet, coat with the olive oil and add the cumin and a good pinch of salt and pepper. Roast in the oven for 40 minutes, turning halfway through. The cauliflower should be slightly golden and softened but with a slight bite.

To make the chimichurri, blend all the ingredients in a food processor, adding olive oil bit by bit, until you get a chunky sauce. Transfer to a bowl or airtight container. Any that you don't use can be kept for up to a week in the refrigerator.

To make the pico de gallo, gently mix the tomatoes and red onion, then mix in the coriander, lemon juice and salt.

To assemble, first lay the cauliflower down, smother with the chimichurri, then load the pico de gallo on top. Sprinkle with pepitas and serve.

CELERIAC/CELERY ROOT WITH MACADAMIA RICOTTA AND PADRÓN PEPPERS

Serves: 4 as a side or 2 as a main   Time: 55 minutes

"Celeriac for me looks like an earth alien," I said. My grandma laughed and told me that until I learned the fruits and vegetables that come from the land my feet walk upon, my connection to nature would only go so far. She would say, "You know the names of fashion brands but do you know the names of the trees and nature's bounty?"

Roasted celeriac is my jam. Try it with a good dollop of macadamia ricotta and you'll be buying all the earth aliens you can find.

This is great served with Spicy Lentils and Beetroot Salad (see page 96). When the wild garlic season hits, I swap the macadamia ricotta for Wild Garlic Pesto (see page 105), as wild garlic really complements the celeriac. A perfect example of how we can mix up a dish by just changing the sauce. Serve with Spicy Lentils And Beetroot/Beets Salad (see page 96) and Boujie Broccli (see page 146) for a banging plant feast.

WHAT YOU'LL NEED

Baking sheet
Blender
Frying pan

INGREDIENTS

1 large celeriac/celery root, peeled and
    sliced lengthways (approx. 1cm/½in thick)
olive oil
160g/5¾oz Padrón peppers
¼ teaspoon dried chilli/hot pepper flakes
a handful of chopped chives
salt and pepper

FOR THE MACADAMIA RICOTTA

150g/5½oz/1 cup macadamias
1 tablespoon nutritional yeast
120ml/4fl oz/½ cup water
2 tablespoons lemon juice
¼ teaspoon salt and pepper
1 tablespoon finely chopped chives

METHOD

Preheat the oven to 200°C/400°F/Gas 6.

Arrange the celeriac/celery root slices on a baking sheet and cover with a good glug of olive oil and a good pinch of salt and pepper. Roast for 40 minutes, turning them over halfway through. You want them to be slightly golden and softened but still with a slight bite.

Meanwhile, blend the macadamias in a blender with the nutritional yeast, lemon juice and salt and pepper, adding the water bit by bit. You want to end up with a smooth mixture. Spoon into a bowl and fold in the chives. If it's too thick and your blender needs a bit of help, add an extra tablespoon of water as you go.

Heat a good glug of olive oil in a frying pan over a medium heat. When the oil is hot, add the Padrón peppers. Cook for a few minutes until slightly charred, then turn them over and cook for a few minutes on the other side. Add salt and pepper and the chilli flakes.

Arrange the cooked celeriac on a serving plate, dollop on the macadamia ricotta, add the Padrón peppers, and sprinkle with the chopped chives.

BANGING BOAT DHAL

Serves: 4 Time: 1 hour

Let's face it, everyone loves a dhal. It's a dish to be shared. I have been making this for years on retreats, for ceremonial supper clubs, for lovers, for friends and for my community. This is my go-to when funds are low but I want to entertain. I used to think that when times are hard, I should stay home alone. Of course that has a place, yet I always remember what an elder, Juan, said to me in Colombia. "You think we only come together to celebrate the joy. No, we celebrate and come together in all the moments, in pain and hardship too. In fact, that is more important because we remember that we are not alone and that we all have times of love and pain. There is connection in this. You have the plants and you have your community, and we can take strength from them both coming together. For all that happens on our journey reminds us to get out of the mind, smile and have a little compassion for others."

This dish has many ancient herbs and spices that all tell a story. Red lentils are said to symbolize the circle of life, a reminder to stay humble and give thanks for what we have. With creamy coconut and a fresh tomato kick, this dish is comforting and so nourishing.

Serve with Ancient Spiced rice (see page 154), Cumin and Garlic Potatoes (see page 146), Raita (see page 153) and Spicy Mango and Palm Heart Salad (see page 98) for a plant feast.

WHAT YOU'LL NEED

Saucepan

INGREDIENTS

2 tablespoons coconut oil

1 white onion, chopped

2 garlic cloves, chopped

1 teaspoon grated root ginger

1 tablespoon garam masala

1 teaspoon ground cumin

½ teaspoon ground coriander

½ teaspoon ground turmeric

a pinch of cayenne pepper (or more depending how spicy you like it)

380g/13oz/2 cups dried red split lentils

1 × 400g/14oz can of chopped tomatoes

1 × 400ml/14fl oz can of coconut milk

825ml/28fl oz/3½ cups water

a large handful of coriander/cilantro leaves, chopped

80g/2¾oz/1 cup spinach leaves, chopped

juice of 1 lemon

salt and pepper

METHOD

Heat the coconut oil in a saucepan over a medium heat and add the onion and garlic. Cook for 5 minutes until the onion starts to soften. Add the ginger, garam masala, cumin, ground coriander, turmeric and cayenne. Keep an eye on the spices and keep stirring so they don't burn.

Add the lentils, then stir for a minute or so to make sure everything is well combined (this is to make the lentils really flavoursome). Add the canned tomatoes and coconut milk, stir, then add the water. Keep stirring so the lentils don't stick to the bottom – this is the trick with dhal. Cook for 10 minutes, then turn the heat down to low and cook for another 30 minutes, stirring often, until it is thick and creamy. Season with a large pinch of salt and pepper.

Add most of the fresh coriander, the spinach and lemon juice, then stir until the spinach has wilted. Taste and add more salt and pepper, if desired. Leave to stand for 10 minutes to allow the banging flavours to develop.

Serve with the remaining fresh coriander scattered on top.

CAULIFLOWER BAKE WITH KALE AND CASHEW CHEESE

Serves: 6   Time: 1 hour + 4–6 hours soaking

When I lived in a raw food community, we would massage kale with our hands for an hour to break down the tough fibres. However, I don't have time to do this, so instead I pulse it in the food processor. It gives the dish a great texture, is easy to digest and children don't notice that they are eating a bowl of greens.

This dish is so comforting. It's inspired by a UK classic – cauliflower cheese – but is lighter and more nourishing. It is best served with Herby Potatoes (see page 144) and Spicy Lentils and Beetroot Salad (See page 96).

WHAT YOU'LL NEED

Baking pan
Food processor
Blender

INGREDIENTS

2 cauliflowers (approx. 500g/1lb 2oz each),
   cut into florets
olive oil
¼ teaspoon salt, plus an extra pinch
150g/5½oz curly kale, tough stalks removed
15g/½oz/½ cup flat leaf parsley leaves

FOR THE CASHEW CHEESE

300g/10½oz/2 cups raw cashews, soaked
   for 4–6 hours, then drained
¼ teaspoon dried chilli/hot pepper flakes
¼ teaspoon black pepper
1 small garlic clove, peeled
1 tablespoon nutritional yeast
2 tablespoons lemon juice
375ml/13fl oz/1½ cups water
250ml/9fl oz/1 cup oat milk
salt and pepper

METHOD

Preheat the oven to 220°C/425°F/Gas 7.

Arrange the cauliflower florets in a baking pan. Add a glug of olive oil and a pinch of salt. Bake for 30 minutes, turning them halfway, until golden and softened but still with some bite.

Pulse the kale, the ¼ teaspoon of salt and the parsley in a food processor until fine.

Blitz all the cashew cheese ingredients in a blender until smooth.

Add the kale to the cauliflower and mix. Pour the cashew cheese over the cauliflower and shake the pan so it's evenly distributed. Place back in the oven and bake for another 20 minutes until lovely and golden on the top.

GNOCCHI WITH TRUFFLE CASHEW CREAM AND CHARRED CAVOLO NERO

Serves: 4   Time: 25 minutes + 4–6 hours soaking

My nan sends handwritten letters to supermarkets, asking them to reduce the amounts of salt and chemicals in their vegan ready meals. She doesn't understand why they are full of all kinds of unnatural things. Vegan food should just be plants that look after the body. I often imagine what the person opening the letters thinks. A 97-year-old woman still so passionate for the health of future generations. She tells me, "We have to look after each other, and stand up for what we believe in. When you live through a war, you soon see that you have to think of the future, but you have to remember you help create it."

This is a super-quick dish that will make you never want to buy a ready meal again. You can leave out the truffle oil, if you like; I got gifted a bottle and I use it sometimes for a bit of a posh vibe.

Serve with a sprinkle of Brazil Nut Parmesan (see page 174) and a Simple Garden Salad (page 101).

WHAT YOU'LL NEED
Blender
Saucepan
Frying pan

INGREDIENTS
2 × 500g/1lb 2oz packs of gnocchi
olive oil
250g/9oz cavolo nero, tough stems
  removed and leaves shredded
salt and pepper

FOR THE TRUFFLE CASHEW CREAM
150g/5½oz/1 cup raw cashews, soaked
  for 4–6 hours, then drained
1 tablespoon nutritional yeast

1 tablespoon truffle oil (optional)
1 tablespoon lemon juice
1 teaspoon garlic granules
¼ teaspoon black peppercorns
¼ teaspoon salt
250ml/9fl oz/1 cup water

METHOD
First, make the truffle cashew cream by blending the soaked cashews, nutritional yeast, truffle oil, lemon juice, garlic granules, black peppercorns and salt in a blender, adding the water bit by bit, until smooth. The cream should

be quite runny at this point, as it will thicken when heated. Set aside.

Cook the gnocchi in a pan of salted boiling water according to the package directions. You will know it's ready when the gnocchi rises to the top of the pan. Drain.

Meanwhile, heat a good glug of olive oil in a frying pan over a medium heat, then add the cavolo nero. Fry for about 5 minutes until the leaves soften and start to char. Turn off the heat and add the cashew cream, stirring well so it doesn't stick to the bottom of the pan. Stir in the gnocchi, then divide between your bowls. Season with salt and pepper and serve.

SMALL PLATES

These are the magic. You can create meals by
mixing and matching a few of these small plates
or serve some alongside a big plate. Make salads
and add a side. Or create a huge feast with many!
There are no rules apart from the ones you make.

THE POTATOES

Potatoes are my FAVOURITE thing. No plant feast is complete without a side of papas. Here are my go-to recipes. Nana B tells me that potatoes are why the UK is still alive. "They are a symbol of love. Everything about the potato is useful; they can last through the harshest winter, and the darkest night, feed the whole street and make the compost thrive."

I never peel potatoes, as the skin is where most of the nutrients are. And it takes less time!

HERBED POTATOES

Serves: 4 as a side
Time: 30 minutes

I cook these fresh and flavoursome potatoes a lot in summer. The tanginess from the mustard works perfectly with the infusion of fresh herbs. Best served with salads or to balance out a heartier plant feast. The herbed cream dressing also works well over green beans, roasted carrots and courgette ribbions.

WHAT YOU'LL NEED
Saucepan

INGREDIENTS
750g/1lb 10oz baby potatoes
FOR THE HERBED CREAM
1 teaspoon wholegrain mustard
1 teaspoon lemon juice
1 garlic clove, crushed
4 tablespoons olive oil
a handful of finely chopped dill
a handful of finely chopped flat leaf parsley leaves
a few mint leaves, finely chopped (swap for wild fennel leaves if in season)
salt

METHOD
Cook the potatoes in a pan of salted boiling water for 15–20 minutes until tender.

Meanwhile, to make the herbed cream, whisk the mustard, lemon juice, garlic, olive oil and a big pinch of salt together in a bowl. When it has reached a creamy consistency, fold in the herbs.

Once the potatoes are cooked, drain and transfer to a serving bowl. Spoon over the herbed cream and mix until well combined. Serve hot or cold.

CUMIN AND GARLIC POTATOES

Serves: 4 as a side
Time: 35 minutes

I have wooed many retreats and dates with these bad boys. Sometimes I just make a bowl of these and eat them on their own. If you have any left over, they're delicious for breakfast the next day, warmed up with a side of fresh avocado and tomatoes.

WHAT YOU'LL NEED

Saucepan
Frying pan

INGREDIENTS

750g/1lb 10oz baby potatoes
olive oil
1 white onion, finely chopped
1 tablespoon cumin seeds
3 garlic cloves, crushed
2 tablespoons lemon juice
50g/1¾oz/1¼ cups coriander/cilantro
    leaves, finely chopped
salt

METHOD

Cook the potatoes in a pan of salted boiling water for about 20 minutes.

Meanwhile, heat a drizzle of olive oil in a frying pan over a medium heat, then add the onion and cumin seeds. Cook for 5 minutes until the onion is softened, then add the garlic.

Drain the potatoes and add to the frying pan. Add a large pinch of salt and cook until the potatoes start to char, then turn and cook the other side. Add the lemon juice, a pinch more salt and coriander and stir. Serve warm.

LAZY LEMON AND THYME ROAST BABY POTATOES

Serves: 4 as a side
Time: 1 hour

Crunchy on the outside, fluffy on the inside and infused with a garlicy lemon vibe. These potatoes are very comforting.

WHAT YOU'LL NEED

Roasting pan

INGREDIENTS

750g/1lb 10oz baby potatoes
3 tablespoons olive oil
1 teaspoon chopped thyme leaves
8 garlic cloves, unpeeled
1 lemon, halved
a few thyme sprigs
salt

METHOD

Preheat the oven to 200°C/400°F/Gas 6.

Arrange the potatoes in a roasting pan. In a bowl, mix the olive oil, thyme leaves and a good pinch of salt. Pour this over the potatoes, then add the garlic cloves, lemon halves and thyme sprigs. Roast for 50 minutes, turning occasionally. Serve hot.

BOUJIE BROCCOLI WITH TAHINI SAUCE

Serves: 4 as a side   Time: 35 minutes

Broccoli doesn't need to be boring. It's delicious when cooked but still with a slight crunch, laid on a bed of spicy, creamy tahini. I use tahini a lot in sauces, as it easily blends with any herbs, making it very versatile.

Broccoli is said to remind us that trees give life, so eat plenty of these mini trees when your nervous system feels like it needs support. When I'm having a hard time, out comes this boujie broccoli to remind me that everything is alright.

WHAT YOU'LL NEED
Baking sheet

INGREDIENTS
1 large head of broccoli or 2 small heads, cut into florets (approx. 400g/14oz/6 cups)

olive oil

1 chilli, deseeded and finely chopped

1 nori sheet (optional)

½ spring onion/scallion, finely sliced

Hemp Seed and Sesame Dukkah, to serve (see page 170)

salt

one sheet of nori (optional)

FOR THE SPICY TAHINI SAUCE
3 tablespoons light tahini

2 tablespoons lemon juice

½ teaspoon garlic granules

a pinch of cayenne pepper

½ teaspoon agave syrup

½ teaspoon ground cumin

2 tablespoons water

salt and pepper

METHOD
Preheat the oven to 200°C/400°F/Gas 6. Arrange the broccoli florets on a baking sheet and add a glug of olive oil and a pinch of salt. Sprinkle over the chilli, then roast for 25 minutes. You want it crispy and slightly charred with a bit of bite.

Meanwhile, make the spicy tahini sauce by mixing all the ingredients together. Add a little more water if it's too thick; you want a smooth, creamy texture.

If using, roll the nori sheet up tightly, then cut with scissors into thin ribbons.

Spoon three quarters of the sauce onto a plate. Stack the broccoli on top, then drizzle over the rest of the sauce. Sprinkle with the spring onions and dukkah. Finish with the nori ribbons, if using.

BRUSSELS SPROUTS WITH COCONUT, POMEGRANATE AND ORANGE ZEST

Serves: 4 as a side   Time: 30 minutes

Learning what grows in season has been a great way for me to connect to the cycles of nature and to connect to myself more deeply. My grandma often tells me that nature gifts exactly what we need at exactly the right time. Some plants come into season as medicine and some to give us a boost in vitamins. Brussels sprouts grow as winter approaches and these little baby cabbages have a good dose of vitamin C, keeping our immune systems healthy in the colder months. Nature always gives us what we need.

Winter is my time to hibernate; it's a time when I say no to going out and get cozy. I make potions, light the fire and get witchy. However, I don't celebrate Christmas these days; instead, I celebrate winter solstice and then party for 10 days straight. This dish was created for this time, to share nature's bounty and honour the light returning with friends and family. It's a balance of earthy seasonal greens with the pomegranate and orange providing a pinch of sunshine.

WHAT YOU'LL NEED
Baking sheet
Frying pan

INGREDIENTS
120g/4¼oz/1 cup pecans
a pinch of cayenne pepper
1 tablespoon tamari
2 tablespoons maple syrup
1 tablespoon olive oil
300g/10½oz Brussels sprouts, washed, trimmed and halved
1 garlic clove, crushed
1 tablespoon lemon juice
a handful of flat leaf parsley leaves,

chopped, plus extra to serve
2 tablespoons pomegranate seeds
½ teaspoon orange zest
salt and pepper

FOR THE WHIPPED COCONUT
125g/4½oz/½ cup coconut yogurt
2 teaspoons light tahini
1 teaspoon lemon juice
1 small garlic clove, crushed
1 teaspoon sumac
¼ teaspoon agave syrup
1 tablespoon roughly chopped mint leaves
a pinch of cayenne pepper
1 teaspoon olive oil
salt and pepper

METHOD

Preheat the oven to 190°C/375°F/Gas 5. Line a baking sheet with baking parchment.

In a bowl, mix the pecans, cayenne, tamari and maple syrup, making sure the pecans are coated. Spread out on the lined baking sheet and bake for 15 minutes. Be careful not to overcook them, as they'll continue to cook and harden a little when out of the oven.

Meanwhile, heat the olive oil in a frying pan over a medium heat, then add the Brussels sprouts. Cook for 15 minutes until they start to turn golden, then add the garlic and lemon juice and cook for a further 5 minutes. The Brussels sprouts should be softened but still with a bite. Add salt and pepper and the parsley.

While the sprouts are cooking, vigorously mix all the ingredients for the whipped coconut together in a bowl using a fork. Season to taste.

Spoon the whipped coconut onto a serving plate, pile the Brussels sprouts on top and scatter over the pomegranate seeds. Break up the pecans and add to the plate, then add a little more salt and pepper and fresh parsley. Sprinkle with the orange zest at the very end when ready to serve.

SIMPLE GREENS

Serves: 4 as a side   Time: 15 minutes

I'm all about the greens, and this no-faff recipe complements any plant feast. It's super quick and gives you a boost of vitamin C. Spring/collard greens are the first tender cabbages of the year and taste slightly sweet, so always a great choice.

WHAT YOU'LL NEED

Frying pan

INGREDIENTS

olive oil
500g/1lb 2oz spring/collard greens, washed and sliced
2 tablespoons lemon juice
salt

METHOD

Heat a splash of olive oil in a frying pan over a low heat, then add the spring greens. Cook for 10 minutes until the greens become a darker shade of green and soften.

Drizzle over the lemon juice and sprinkle with salt. Serve hot.

BAKED SQUASH WITH CHIMICHURRI

Serves: 4 as a side   Time: 40 minutes

When squash season hits, it's a sign that autumn is here. This dish represents nature turning from green to orange. It's a time of transition and, for me, it's a reminder to bring more stillness into my life.

My nan always asks me around this time, "What is something that gave you comfort that you are now letting go of?" Nature sheds and I follow her lead. The leaf found comfort in the tree branch, but now gracefully reminds itself that it's time to leave.

Chimichurri is great to have to hand. If I have some on-their-way-out herbs, I always blend them with spices and oils. It saves money, and you have a sauce that lasts for a week or so in the refrigerator that complements most roasted vegetables. This dish is a fusion of Latin spices and English seasons – it's basically a dish that sums up my previous marriage.

I like to leave the skin on the squash for this one, as it provides a really nice colour contrast, and there's lots of vitamins in the skin.

WHAT YOU'LL NEED
Baking pan
Food processor

INGREDIENTS
1 acorn squash (approx. 900g/2lb) (or you can use any squash), deseeded and cut into 2.5cm/1in moons
olive oil
juice of ½ lemon
salt and pepper

FOR THE CHIMICHURRI
½ teaspoon dried chilli/hot pepper flakes
2 jalapeños, deseeded and roughly chopped
1 garlic clove, peeled
2 tablespoons lemon juice
¼ teaspoon ground cumin
40g/1½oz/1 cup parsley leaves
40g/1½oz/1 cup coriander/cilantro leaves
a small handful of mint leaves
6 tablespoons olive oil
¼ teaspoon salt
a pinch of black pepper

METHOD
Preheat the oven to 200°C/400°F/Gas 6.

Arrange the squash in a baking pan and add a good glug of olive oil and a good pinch of salt and pepper. Mix to coat the squash, then roast for about 30 minutes until golden and softened but still with a bit of bite.

Meanwhile, blend all the ingredients for the chimichurri in a food processor until well combined and the sauce resembles a pesto.

Layer the squash on a large serving plate so it's overlapping, then cover with the chimichurri. Squeeze over the lemon juice and sprinkle with salt, then serve.

RAITA

Serves: 4 as a side   Time: 15 minutes

Fresh and calming. I always pair this with something spicy, to balance the dishes of a plant feast.

INGREDIENTS
1 cucumber, grated
1 garlic clove, grated
¼ teaspoon salt
¼ teaspoon black pepper
2 tablespoons lemon juice
250g/9oz/1 cup yogurt (I like coconut yogurt)
1 teaspoon grated root ginger
20g/¾oz/½ cup flat leaf parsley leaves, finely chopped
10g/¼oz/¼ cup mint leaves, finely chopped
2 teaspoons olive oil

METHOD
Squeeze the excess water out of the grated cucumber using your hands, then place in a bowl. Add the rest of the ingredients and mix well. Taste and season with a little more salt and pepper, if desired, then serve.

ANCIENT SPICED RICE

Serves: 6 as a side   Time: 35 minutes

Rice is an ancient grain that a large part of the world lives off and has done for thousands of years. It has been offered during prayers and ceremonies. When we were with the elders in the jungle, we would offer rice to the Earth on full moons and new moons to say thank you for all that she gives, for good luck for the next cycle, not just for the land but for our internal selves too.

While living in the community, I would make the food most days, creating dishes with plants, but my rice game was bad – every time I tried to cook it, it just turned to gloop. I would always be so embarrassed. My then husband would say it's okay, that I will master it one day. He would tell me that you can't rush rice. That you have to steam it for 10 minutes after it has been cooked and the water has evaporated, but the secret is not to look at it while it steams. I replied, "Not look at it, why? I wanna see how it's doing!" (I can be quite impatient sometimes). "Things work better when you detach from the outcome. You allow space for things to work out on their own." he said. The words landed and I knew then that this rice method should be applied to many aspects of my life.

This rice is healing and nourishing, a blend of cultures, herbs and spices.

WHAT YOU'LL NEED

Saucepan
Large frying pan

INGREDIENTS

350g/12oz/2 cups white basmati rice
1.25l/3 pints/5 cups water
1 tablespoon coconut oil
2 garlic cloves, crushed
1 tablespoon grated root ginger
1 tablespoon mustard seeds
1 red pepper, deseeded and finely chopped
2 carrots, grated (1 cup grated)
½ teaspoon ground cumin
170g/6oz/1 cup fresh or frozen peas
1 small red chilli, finely chopped (or more

if you like spice)
1 tablespoon ground turmeric
a handful of coriander/cilantro leaves, chopped, plus extra to serve
40g/1½ oz/½ cup coconut flakes, plus 1 tablespoon extra to serve
juice of 1 lemon
salt and pepper
1 tablespoon black sesame seeds, to serve

METHOD

Put the rice in a saucepan with the water and a pinch of salt, then bring to the boil. Turn the heat down and simmer for about 12 minutes, then once all the water has been absorbed,

remove from the heat, place the lid on the pan and leave to steam for 10 minutes.

Meanwhile, heat the coconut oil in a frying pan over a medium heat, then add the garlic, ginger and mustard seeds. Cook for a couple of minutes, then add the red pepper and carrots and cook for 5 minutes, stirring regularly, until the pepper starts to soften. Add a pinch of salt and pepper, the cumin, peas and chilli and cook for a further 5 minutes. Turn the heat down to low and add the rice and the turmeric. Stir well until all the turmeric is combined. Turn the heat off and stir in the coriander, coconut and lemon juice. Season with salt and pepper.

Serve sprinkled with fresh coriander leaves, coconut flakes and the black sesame seeds.

SIMPLICITY IN PLANTAIN

Serves: 4 as a side   Time: 10 minutes

My tip when it comes to plantain is to use ones that are yellow but with some brown spots, as these will gift the sweetness. Green plantain is more savoury.

WHAT YOU'LL NEED
Frying pan

INGREDIENTS
1 tablespoon coconut oil
2 plantains, sliced

METHOD
Heat the coconut oil in a frying pan over a low heat, then add the plantain slices. Fry on both sides until golden.

Serve hot.

PEA AND MINT HUMMUS

Serves: 6 as a side   Time: 10 minutes

Packed full of protein, this is a hummus that gives you energy. A dip that you don't have to spend loads of money on. This recipe is a retreat classic, with a delicate mint flavour and creamy texture.

I grow herbs on my boat roof, which is how I learned what herbs grow seasonally. It's a really inexpensive way to elevate the dishes you create.

WHAT YOU'LL NEED
Food processor

INGREDIENTS
250g/9oz/2 cups fresh or frozen peas

1 × 400g/14oz can of chickpeas/garbanzo beans, drained and rinsed

½ teaspoon salt

¼ teaspoon black pepper

½ teaspoon ground cumin

1 garlic clove, crushed

3 tablespoons lemon juice

2 tablespoons light tahini

a pinch of cayenne pepper

3 tablespoons olive oil, plus extra to finish

1 tablespoon chopped mint leaves, plus extra to garnish

Hemp Seed and Sesame Seed Dukkah, to garnish (see page 170)

METHOD
If using frozen peas, place them in a bowl of warm water for a few minutes until they defrost, then drain and tip into a food processor.

Blend the peas, chickpeas, salt, pepper, cumin, garlic, lemon juice, tahini, cayenne, olive oil and mint leaves in a food processor for a few minutes until smooth. You may need to add a little water to make it come together. Add a little more salt and pepper to taste, if needed. Scatter with some chopped fresh mint, dukkah and a drizzle of olive oil before serving.

WALNUT AND ROASTED RED PEPPER DIP

Serves: 4 as a side   Time: 10 minutes

The sweet flavour of the roasted red peppers combined with the earthy flavour of the walnuts, with a kick from the chilli, means this dip hits all the spots.

Walnuts look like a brain and are really good for the brain. Sometimes nature shows us what parts of the body foods are good for.

I like to serve this with fresh cucumber slices.

WHAT YOU'LL NEED
Food processor

INGREDIENTS
450g/1lb jar of roasted red peppers, drained
1 teaspoon ground cumin
½ teaspoon dried chilli/hot pepper flakes
180g/6¼oz/1½ cups walnuts
½ tablespoon lemon juice
2 tablespoons olive oil
¼ teaspoon salt
½ teaspoon garlic granules
1 teaspoon chopped thyme leaves

METHOD
Blend all the ingredients together in a food processor until smooth, then serve.

ROASTED CARROT AND FENNEL WITH CORIANDER TAHINI CREAM

Serves: 4 as a side   Time: 45 minutes

I remember the first time I pulled carrots from the ground. Growing up as a city kid, I never knew how to grow food or thought about food coming from the earth. Yet here I was at 23, harvesting carrots I'd sown with my own hands and then creating a recipe with them. My friend Kitzia laughed at me. I was shouting in pure joy, "Can you believe I grew these carrots!" Hands flapping in the air. (If you know me, you'll know I'm a bit of a flapper.) When I made this dish and we sat around the table, Kitzia said, "You know, Francesca, everything you have been searching for is under your feet. The Western world tends to search for connection in material things. When you connect with the earth daily, it brings so much joy, a joy that no external thing can ever give. This connection is already inside of you; you just need to spend time with her and rebuild your relationship."

This dish is colourful and takes me back to this memory. When I returned to London, I recreated this dish and added roasted fennel for a sweet aniseed flavour, just to give it that extra depth. Every time I eat a carrot, I think of how just one vegetable can invite us to connect deeper with the land.

WHAT YOU'LL NEED

Roasting pan

Blender

INGREDIENTS

350g/12oz carrots, halved lengthways

2 fennel bulbs (approx. 350g/12oz), quartered

olive oil

1 tablespoon Hemp Seed and Sesame Dukkah (see page 170)

a handful of mint leaves, chopped

salt and pepper

FOR THE CORIANDER TAHINI CREAM

5 tablespoons light tahini

2.5cm/1in piece of root ginger, peeled and grated

a small handful of coriander/cilantro leaves

2 tablespoons lemon juice

¼ teaspoon ground cumin

1 small chilli

125ml/4fl oz/½ cup water

1 tablespoon agave syrup

a pinch of salt

METHOD

Preheat the oven to 200°C/400°F/Gas 6.

Arrange the carrots and fennel in a roasting pan and add a good glug of olive oil and a good pinch of salt and pepper. Mix to coat all the veggies, then roast for 35–40 minutes until softened and slightly golden.

Meanwhile, blend all the ingredients for the coriander tahini cream in a blender until you get a smooth, creamy green sauce. If it feels too thick, add an extra tablespoon of water at a time.

To assemble, spoon the cream onto a serving plate in the middle. Stack the roasted veg on top, creating height. Scatter over the hemp seed dukkah, then sprinkle with fresh coriander for some colour. Season with salt and pepper and serve.

ASPARAGUS WITH SMOKED GARLIC CASHEW CREAM

Serves: 4 as a side   Time: 20 minutes + 4–6 hours soaking

I love the faint bitterness of asparagus drizzled with the sweet garlic cashew cream. The perfect balance.

They say that asparagus was used in lust and fertility spells, especially when it came to men's stamina and potency. Asparagus comes into season just as mating season starts.

This dish was created as the sunsets became later in the day. Boat jams on the roof, potions and a few sides with friends. It represents the start of a summer of love.

WHAT YOU'LL NEED

Blender
Frying pan

INGREDIENTS

olive oil
300g/10½oz asparagus, trimmed
a handful of Brazil Nut Parmesan
   (see page 174)
salt and pepper

FOR THE SMOKED GARLIC CASHEW CREAM

100g/3½oz/¾ cup cashews, soaked
   for 4–6 hours, then drain
1 tablespoon nutritional yeast
½ teaspoon smoked garlic granules
¼ teaspoon salt
2 tablespoons lemon juice
a pinch of black pepper
125ml/4fl oz/½ cup water

METHOD

Blend all the ingredients for the cashew cream in a blender until you get a really smooth, creamy consistency. If it's still a little thick, add an extra tablespoon of water at a time.

Heat a drizzle of olive oil in a frying pan over a medium heat, then add the asparagus. Cook for about 7 minutes, turning occasionally, until slightly charred and softened but still with a slight bite.

Arrange the asparagus on a plate and drizzle over the cashew cream. Sprinkle with the Brazil Nut Parmesan and season with salt and pepper.

BUTTER BEANS WITH A SPICY ZING

Serves: 4 as a side   Time: 15 minutes

I was told that chillies are medicine, that they can assist in bringing passion and awaken the inner creative fire inside. Although, let's remember that no two chillies are the same. Some have a larger punch than others.

This dish is fire and spicy, with lots of herbs and a zesty vibe from the lemon. Perfect for dunking into or to complement a salad.

WHAT YOU'LL NEED
Frying pan

INGREDIENTS
3 tablespoons olive oil

1 large chilli, finely chopped

3 garlic gloves, crushed

1 × 400g/14oz can of butter/lima beans, drained and rinsed

1½ tablespoons za'atar

150g/5½oz/1¼ cups cherry tomatoes, halved

a handful of flat leaf parsley leaves, chopped, plus extra to serve

1 tablespoon lemon juice

1 teaspoon lemon zest

salt and pepper

METHOD
Heat the olive oil in a frying pan over a medium heat, then add the chilli and garlic. Cook for a couple of minutes, then add the butter beans, za'atar and tomatoes. Season with a large pinch of salt and pepper and stir.

Add the parsley leaves, lemon juice and lemon zest. Stir for 10 minutes until the tomatoes are softened but still with a bit of bite.

Season with a little more black pepper, then serve sprinkled with fresh parsley.

SPRINKLE OF BITS

Let me tell you this: to elevate a plant dish, it's all about the sprinkle of bits! These are great on top of salads, plates and soups and even sometimes on desserts. They give a crunch, which mixes up the textures. A reminder: a dish doesn't always need a sprinkle of bits, but it will give that extra vibe.

HEMP SEED AND SESAME DUKKAH

Makes: 1 small jar   Time: 10 minutes

Dukkah is a blend of nuts, seeds and spices used as a garnish in the Middle East. After playing around with many flavours, I knew I had to add the mighty hemp seed into the mix. Full of protein, this seed gives a good crunch, and when paired with cumin and coriander, it has a sweet, warming, earthy bite.

WHAT YOU'LL NEED
Pestle and mortar (I use a pebble and bowl if you don't have one of these)

WHAT YOU'LL NEED
Frying pan

INGREDIENTS
1 tablespoon cumin seeds
2 tablespoons coriander seeds
¼ teaspoon cayenne pepper
1 teaspoon salt
45g/1½oz/¼ cup hemp seeds
4 tablespoons sesame seeds

METHOD
In a hot frying pan, dry-fry the cumin seeds and coriander seeds until fragrant, around a couple of minutes. Transfer to a pestle and mortar and grind until you get a sandy texture, then tip into a bowl and add the cayenne and salt.

Toast the hemp seeds and the sesame seeds in a frying pan over a medium heat for 3 minutes until slightly browned, then transfer to the bowl with the cumin mixture. Mix until well combined. Leave to cool.

Store in an airtight container or jar for up to 3 months.

WALNUT AND FENNEL SEED DUKKAH

Makes: 1 small jar   Time: 15 minutes

Walnuts are good for the brain, and when warmed, they taste slightly buttery. The fennel then adds a slight zest and the pinch of spice brings out the passion. This sprinkle of bits hits all the notes and works well with salads and on top of saucy roasted veg.

WHAT YOU'LL NEED
Pestle and mortar (I use a pebble and bowl if you don't have one of these)

WHAT YOU'LL NEED
Frying pan

INGREDIENTS
1 tablespoon fennel seeds
2 tablespoons cumin seeds
90g/3¼oz/¾ cup walnuts
45g/1½oz/¼ cup hemp seeds
1 teaspoon salt
¼ teaspoon cayenne pepper

METHOD
In a hot frying pan, dry-fry the fennel seeds and cumin seeds until fragrant and slightly browned, about 2 minutes. Transfer to a pestle and mortar and grind until you get a sandy texture, then tip into a bowl.

Toast the walnuts in the frying pan over a medium heat for a few minutes until slightly browned. Be careful they don't burn. Stay on close watch. Transfer to the pestle and mortar and grind until they look like sand, although it's okay if there are a few larger bits. Add to the bowl with the fennel and cumin seeds.

Toast the hemp seeds in the frying pan over a medium heat for 2 minutes until slightly browned, then add to the bowl. Stir well, then add the salt and cayenne pepper and mix. Leave to cool.

Store in an airtight container or jar for up to 3 months.

TAMARI SPICED ALMONDS

Makes: 1 small jar   Time: 20 minutes

With a serious crunch that's both sweet and spicy, you can eat these tamari spiced almonds alone or add them to salads or any dish for a tamari hit.

WHAT YOU'LL NEED
Baking sheet

INGREDIENTS
150g/5½oz/1 cup whole almonds
2 tablespoons tamari
¼ teaspoon cayenne pepper
2 tablespoons maple syrup

METHOD
Preheat the oven to 200°C/400°F/ Gas 6. Line a baking sheet with baking parchment.

Mix the almonds, tamari, cayenne and maple syrup in a bowl until well combined. Leave for 5 minutes, stirring occasionally. Spread the almonds out on the lined baking sheet, then bake for 6–8 minutes, keeping an eye on them so they don't burn. Remove from the oven and set aside to cool; they will harden up more as they do.

These will last for up to 2 weeks in an airtight container or jar.

BRAZIL NUT PARMESAN

Makes: 1 small jar   Time: 10 minutes

This was one of the first things I started making when I was on my raw food flex. It adds depth to any dish – not only does the crumble texture look beautiful, the garlic edge complements anything roasted or fried. I love to slice tomatoes and sprinkle this parmesan on top – it can be as simple as that.

WHAT YOU'LL NEED
Food processor

INGREDIENTS
130g/4½oz/1 cup Brazil nuts
1 teaspoon chopped garlic
¼ teaspoon salt
1 tablespoon nutritional yeast

METHOD
Pulse all the ingredients together in a food processor until you get a fine crumble. Taste and add more salt, if desired.

Store in an airtight container or jar in the refrigerator for up to 3 months.

SWEET AND SUPER SPICY COCONUT PEPITAS

Makes: 1 small jar   Time: 15 minutes

These pepitas are banging, although they may not last long especially if, like me, you eat them by the handful. I often throw these on top of my main or side plates to add a little extra flavour. Both spicy and zesty, the coconut finds balance between the two.

WHAT YOU'LL NEED

Baking sheet

INGREDIENTS

180g/6¼oz/1 cup pumpkin seeds/pepitas

½ teaspoon salt

¼ teaspoon cayenne pepper

2 teaspoons unsweetened desiccated/
   dried shredded coconut

½ teaspoon medium curry powder

1 tablespoon lime juice

2 teaspoons maple syrup

METHOD

Preheat the oven to 200°C/400°F/ Gas 6. Line a baking sheet with baking parchment.

Mix all the dry ingredients in a bowl first, then add the lime juice and maple syrup. Spread the mixture out on a baking sheet, then bake in the oven for 12 minutes until slightly golden on top. Leave to cool.

Store in an airtight container or jar for up to a month.

DESSERTS AND SWEET THINGS

Let's face it, cakes and sweet things are a love story of their own. One of my first side hustles was selling plant-based cakes. I loved seeing people be like, are these really all from plants? You know they're hitting all the spots when people don't even realize that what they're eating is good for them.

All these desserts are raw and vegan. They can be kept in the refrigerator for up to a week or in the freezer for up to a month. So if you're not like me and are able to eat only a slice or two, then you can keep any leftovers on hand for when the need for something sweet calls.

WILD ORANGE GANACHE TART

**Serves: 12   Time: 25 minutes + 45 minutes in the freezer
or 3 hours to set in the refrigerator**

You can make this tart without the orange oil, but it tastes like Terry's chocolate orange with it! Dark chocolate with sunshine feels.

WHAT YOU'LL NEED
Food processor
23cm/9in loose-bottomed tart pan

INGREDIENTS
250g/9oz/1¾ cups cashews
a pinch of salt
225g/8oz/1½ cups pitted dates, chopped
    (I use deglet noor as they are cheaper
    than medjool dates)
¼ teaspoon ground ginger
2 tablespoons cacao powder
1 teaspoon coconut oil, melted

FOR THE FILLING
180ml/6fl oz/¾ cup melted coconut oil
280ml/9½fl oz/scant 1¼ cups maple syrup
125g/1½oz/1¼ cups cacao powder
4 drops of food-grade orange oil

METHOD
To make the tart base, pulse the cashews, salt, dates, ginger and cacao powder in a food processor until the cashews and dates have broken down and the mixture is starting to stick together. Add the melted coconut oil and blend for a minute or so more until a dough forms. Spoon the dough into the tart pan and press down firmly to cover the bottom and sides.

To make the filling, mix together the melted coconut oil and maple syrup in a bowl, then add the cacao powder and whisk with a fork until smooth. Add the orange oil. Stir and then pour the mixture into the tart pan, giving the pan a little shake so the filling is evenly distributed. Make sure you get the filling in quickly, as the coconut oil hardens as it cools so it will be harder to pour.

Place the tart in the refrigerator for 3 hours or in the freezer for 45 minutes to set. If frozen it needs to thaw at room temperature before cutting and serving.

CHOCOLATE-DUNKED STRAWBERRIES

Serves: 3–4 Time: 15 minutes + 20 minutes to set in the refrigerator

These are real easy to make. The sweetness of the strawberries smothered in dark chocolate is the perfect balance, and they just make your heart feel good.

Chocolate strawberries are a symbol of love. This recipe was created on the boat, when strawberry season was in full swing. They were shared out at my full moon circle. Comments of romance were the thing.

In all honesty, I believe we should bring romance into everything we do. I make chocolate strawberries for me and share them with friends, coz let's face it, friends are soulmates too.

WHAT YOU'LL NEED

Saucepan

INGREDIENTS

50g/1¾oz coconut oil
85ml/3fl oz/⅓ cup maple syrup
30g/1oz/⅓ cup cacao powder
1 punnet of strawberries (approx. 230g/8oz)

METHOD

Place a sheet of baking parchment over a large plate and set aside.

Fill a saucepan with about 2.5cm/1in of water, then place it over a low heat.

Place a heatproof glass bowl over the pan and add the coconut oil. Stir occasionally until it has melted. Add the maple syrup and stir well, then add the cacao powder bit by bit, stirring well so there are no lumps.

Once everything is combined, turn the heat off. Hold a strawberry by its leafy top and dunk it in the chocolate so that it's covered. Place it on the lined plate and repeat with the rest of the strawberries. Put into the refrigerator for 20 minutes to set.

Notes...

You've got to move quick when working with melted chocolate, as it will thicken and harden quickly once it cools down. If you try to reheat it, it can separate.

WILD BLUEBERRY CHEESECAKE

Serves: 12   Time: 25 minutes + 4–6 hours soaking + 3 hours to set in the freezer or overnight in the refrigerator

This cheesecake represents the pure joy of nature. Every time I share this dish, people always ask if the colour is natural. The wild blueberry, with all its revitalizing power, nourishes the body and makes the spirit smile.

The ginger and coconut base complements the fruity berry cheesecake filling perfectly. It's an ideal dessert for summer, or even when the days are grey and you want something that will just brighten up your day.

WHAT YOU'LL NEED

Food processor
23cm/9in loose-bottomed tart pan
Blender

INGREDIENTS

280g/10oz/scant 2 cups cashews
1 teaspoon ground ginger
180g/6¼oz/1¼ cups pitted dates, chopped
   (I use deglet noor)
40g/1½oz/½ cup unsweetened
   desiccated/dried shredded coconut
a pinch of salt
½ tablespoon coconut oil, melted

FOR THE FILLING

350g/12oz/scant 2½ cups cashews, soaked
   for 4–6 hours, then drained
150g/5½oz/1 cup frozen wild blueberries,
   defrosted
6 tablespoons maple syrup (or agave syrup)
½ teaspoon nutritional yeast
1 teaspoon lemon juice
250ml/9fl oz/1 cup water
8 tablespoons coconut oil, melted

METHOD

To make the base, pulse the cashews, ginger, dates, desiccated coconut and salt in a food processor until broken down, then add the melted coconut oil and blend until the mixture is starting to stick together and form a dough. Spoon the dough into the tart pan, pressing down firmly to cover the bottom.

To make the filling, blend the soaked cashews, wild blueberries, maple syrup, nutritional yeast and lemon juice in the blender, adding the water bit by bit. You want a thick, smooth consistency. If the filling is too thick, add another tablespoon of water. Add the melted coconut oil and blend until well combined.

Pour the filling into the tart pan. Place in the freezer for a minimum of 3 hours or in the refrigerator overnight. If frozen it needs to thaw at room temperature before cutting and serving.

PASSION FRUIT AND COCONUT TART

Serves: 12   Time: 25 minutes + 4–6 hours soaking + 3 hours to set in the freezer or overnight in the refrigerator

When I shared this dessert at one of my ceremonial supper clubs, someone asked, "Is this just made of plants?" I replied, "Of course. Plants that nourish deep and flavours that make you want to move your feet."

A guest called Simone said they'd stopped eating cake, as they wanted to lose weight. That their whole life they've felt this pressure to be a certain size. A man called Leon spoke up and explained how men feel the pressure to look a certain way too. The table was in awe of this man speaking his truth with such vulnerability. We all discussed the pressure of society and adverts showing us what a body should look like. As we ate the cake, a man called Juan proposed that if we ate healthier and connected deeper to ourselves, our focus would be on our mind and how that impacts our body and life, and not on our size or appearance.

I replied, "Yeah, fuck this idea of perfection, nature is full of imperfection and we think it's beautiful; in fact, the imperfection is what makes it beautiful." A woman called Abigail said, "And having to shave my armpits all the time because that's defined as beauty, why?" It felt like we were starting a revolution from this tiny boat. We were all strangers that had connected on the subject of the social pressure of bodies being "perfect", yet we had come from all walks of life. Juan spoke: "It's funny, I came on this boat thinking I'm so different from all of you, yet now I see so many reflections in each one of you."

WHAT YOU'LL NEED
Food processor
23cm/9in loose-bottomed tart pan
blender

INGREDIENTS
250g/9oz/1¾ cups cashews
140g/5oz/1 cup pitted dates
   (I use deglet noor)
½ teaspoon coconut oil, melted

FOR THE FILLING
2 passion fruits
190g/6¾oz/1½ cups cashews, soaked
   for 4–6 hours, then drained
125ml/4fl oz/½ cup water
3 tablespoons agave syrup
6 tablespoons coconut butter, melted
   (this is found in all health food shops;
   it's richer than coconut oil, but if you can't
   find this, then opt for coconut oil)

METHOD

To make the base, pulse the cashews and dates in a food processor until broken down, then add the melted coconut oil and blend for a few minutes until well combined and the mixture is starting to stick together and form a kind of dough. Spoon the mixture into the tart pan and press down firmly to cover the bottom and sides.

To make the filling, halve the passion fruits and spoon the insides into the blender. Add the soaked cashews, water and agave and blend until really smooth. If the filling is too thick, add another tablespoon of water. Add the melted coconut butter and blend until well combined.

Pour the mixture into the tart pan, giving it a shake so it's evenly distributed. Place in the freezer for 3 hours or in the refrigerator overnight to set. If frozen it needs to thaw at room temperature before cutting and serving.

CACAO AND PEANUT SWIRL CAKE

Serves: 12   Time: 35 minutes + 4 hours soaking + 3 hours to set in the freezer or overnight in the refrigerator

This is a dessert that I created on a retreat, where the sea and its dancing waves inspired the cake's swirls. Sweet but salty, with a vanilla and peanut taste.

My grandma tells me often that when fear captures me or I feel overwhelmed, to sit with water, to get inspired by it. She tells me that water can be strong and delicate at the same time; it moves around obstacles gently, it doesn't fear where it's going, it doesn't get caught up in the future, it just adapts to what is in its way. Water reminds me to flow in life, and when I'm in flow mode, I create.

WHAT YOU'LL NEED

Food processor
23cm/9in loose-bottomed cake pan
Blender

INGREDIENTS

160g/5¾oz/1 cup whole almonds
160g/5¾oz/¾ cup pitted dates (I use
    deglet noor, as they are cheaper than
    medjool dates)
a pinch of salt
½ teaspoon coconut oil, melted

FOR THE FILLING

250g/9oz/1¾ cups cashews, soaked
    for 4–6 hours, then drained

WHITE PART

125g/4½oz/½ cup peanut butter
2 drops of pure vanilla extract
4 tablespoons agave syrup
250ml/9fl oz/1 cup water
5 tablespoons coconut oil, melted

DARK PART

a large pinch of salt
3 tablespoons agave syrup
250ml/9fl oz/1 cup water
5 tablespoons cacao powder
4 tablespoons coconut oil, melted

METHOD

To make the base, pulse the almonds
and dates in a food processor until
broken down, then add the salt and
melted coconut oil and blend for a few
minutes until well combined and the
mixture is starting to stick together.
Spoon the mixture into the tart pan and
press down firmly to cover the bottom.
To make the filling, divide the soaked
cashews in half and place one half in
the blender with the peanut butter,
vanilla extract, agave and water and
blend until smooth. If the filling is too
thick and isn't coming together, add an
extra tablespoon of water at a time. Add
the melted coconut oil and blend until
well combined. Transfer the mixture
to a jar or bowl and set aside while you
make the chocolate filling.

Blend the other half of the soaked
cashews in the food processor with
the salt, agave, water and cacao powder
until smooth. If the filling is too thick
and isn't coming together, add an extra
tablespoon of water at a time. Add
the melted coconut oil and blend
until combined.

Pour some of the chocolate filling into
the tart pan to create a circle, then pour
some of the peanut filling on top, and
repeat until both are used up. Use a
chopstick to create swirls in the filling.

Place in the freezer for 3 hours or in the
refrigerator overnight to set. If frozen
it needs to thaw at room temperature
before cutting and serving.

POTIONS

My tonics and potions are full of herbs that heal and herbs that feel. These potions have changed my life and helped me channel my inner witch/wizard inside.

In this section, you'll discover how to reinvent tea and pimp up your hot chocolate into something that will lift your spirit, build your immune system and work with your body wherever you are at.

Whether you need energy, calming or something in between, this section is for taking your mind, body and spirit to the next level. These potions are full of superfoods, adaptogens, medicinal mushrooms and magic.

There is something for everyone, from my famous Cosmic Chocolate Potion (see page 191), to my Stay Up Till Sunrise Potion (see page 193) and my Chill the Fuck Out Potion (See page 194). There are potions for lovemaking and potions to soothe after a wild night.

My journey to learning about these herbs has taken over a decade. I've travelled far and wide and spent time where these precious plants grow, from cacao farms in Colombia to ginger farms in India. I've learned how to take care of them from their caretakers, the grandfathers and grandmothers of the lands. Yet it all started with my own grandmother. Every time I would go to her house she'd ask, "Would you like a chicory tea, Francesca?" When you are seven years old, chicory tea is not what you want. And yet, although I didn't know it then, she planted the seed for my love of plants. She was pretty radical for her time.

My love for herbs, tonics and potions came a lot later. My potions are inspired by jungle living, with wisdom from my grandma's plant knowledge and my own extra magic. I believe in the power of these blends I have created and have seen many people be amazed by my herbal highs that have kept them dancing all night till sunrise. These potions are ultimately a love story to the Earth. I hope they give you as much love as they have me.

Take a moment before drinking these powerful herbs!

COSMIC CHOCOLATE POTION

Makes: 1 mug   Time: 5 minutes

This beautiful blend gives your immune system a warm embrace. Cacao for the heart and reishi for the body, combined, provide the essence to elevate your mood. It provides healing on all the levels, whether that is physical, spiritual, emotional or mental. A mug a day is all you need for your daily ritual of self-care. Magic in a mug.

WHAT YOU'LL NEED

Saucepan

INGREDIENTS

1 mug of plant milk (whatever mug you will be drinking from)

1 tablespoon cacao powder

1 teaspoon coconut sugar, plus extra to serve if desired

a pinch of ground cinnamon

½ teaspoon reishi mushroom powder

¼ teaspoon ground ginger

dried rose petals, to serve (optional)

METHOD

Heat the plant milk in a saucepan over a medium heat (do not bring to the boil), then add the rest of the ingredients (except the rose petals, if using), whisking together until hot and well combined.

Add additional coconut sugar and rose petals as desired, then serve.

STAY UP TILL SUNRISE POTION

Makes: 1 mug   Time: 5 minutes

When I returned from the jungle, I had changed. The life I knew before still existed, but I wasn't the same. My addiction, which had been so much a part of me, no longer controlled me, and my connection to the scene had changed.

Yet my passion for dancing and parties still remained.

The question was, how was I gonna be able to keep up with my mates? So, I lit my fire and channelled that inner witch. I created this stay up till sunrise potion. It tastes delicious and gives me a little extra energy to shake my arse to a funky beat, dance all day at festivals and still have energy. I usually drink a litre of this daily while playing in the fields at festivals, and a few extra mugs if I need some help staying up till sunrise. My friends, well, they do them and I do me. These days, I party a little differently. I'll always be at the front of the dance floor, bare foot, flask in hand, sipping on my potion, making moves. Dancing for me always shifts my mood. I'm not gonna lie, people come up to me and ask if I am high. Nah, bruv, I'm high on life with some help from my plant allies.

I remember my nan's words: "Dancing is a form of prayer. Shake off the energy; give back to the Earth what no longer serves. It's what we have been doing since the beginning of time."

WHAT YOU'LL NEED
Saucepan

INGREDIENTS
1 mug of plant milk (whatever mug you will be drinking from)

3 tablespoons cacao powder

1 teaspoon maca powder

a large pinch of cayenne pepper

1 teaspoon coconut sugar

a pinch of ground allspice

METHOD
Heat the plant milk in a saucepan over a medium heat (do not bring to the boil), then add all the other ingredients, whisking together until hot and well combined. Add extra coconut sugar as desired before serving.

GRANDMA'S CHICORY (AKA CHILL THE FUCK OUT) POTION

Makes: 1 mug   Time: 5 minutes

Chicory/Belgian endive reminds me of my grandmother. It was always sitting there on the shelf and she would make it every morning without fail. I used to think she was so weird. It wasn't until I was much older that I understood chicory, and that her weirdness was, in fact, her wisdom.

Chicory is a plant that looks after the liver. Combined with ashwagandha, it helps to soothe the nervous system – calmness in a mug. I sip this potion when I'm trying to sleep after a wild night out. I give it to friends when they are having trouble with their mental health. I share it at festivals, as it really does assist in chilling the fuck out. Deliciously creamy with a malty flavour.

WHAT YOU'LL NEED
Saucepan

INGREDIENTS
1 mug of plant milk (whatever mug you will be drinking from)

1 teaspoon chicory/Belgian endive powder

½ teaspoon ashwagandha powder

a pinch of allspice

1 teaspoon coconut sugar, plus extra to serve

METHOD
Heat the plant milk in a saucepan over a medium heat (do not bring to the boil), then add the rest of the ingredients, whisking together until hot and well combined.

Add additional coconut sugar as desired, then serve.

SUNSHINE POTION

Makes: 1 mug   Time: 5 minutes + 1 hour stewing

A potion that represents the sun and gives life force. It's perfect for when the immune system needs a little extra TLC, or for those cold days where you want to feel the internal rays.

Turmeric is known for its anti-inflammatory properties. In this potion, it's blended with ginger and cayenne for a slight fiery punch to complement the earthy scent.

WHAT YOU'LL NEED

Saucepan
Teapot (optional)

INGREDIENTS

1 mug of plant milk (whatever mug you will be drinking from; I like almond milk for this)
1 teaspoon grated root ginger (or you can use ½ teaspoon ground ginger)
½ teaspoon ground cinnamon
a pinch of black pepper
1 teaspoon ground turmeric
¼ teaspoon ground cardamom
a pinch of cayenne pepper
1 teaspoon coconut sugar

METHOD

Heat the plant milk in a saucepan over a medium heat (do not bring to the boil), then add the rest of the ingredients, whisking until hot and well combined.

I really enjoy the warm tiny bits of ginger, but if you like, you can pass the potion through a sieve/fine-mesh strainer before serving.

I like to double this up and leave in a teapot over the wood burner for 1 hour, so it brews slowly. Just like ancient times.

MACA ROSE: A GENTLE LOVE POTION

Makes: 1 mug   Time: 5 minutes

Maca to give a little extra energy while balancing hormones and awakening passion. Rose to bring love and a calming effect on the nervous system while gently assisting the opening of the heart. A pinch of cayenne pepper to ignite the creative fire.

Rose is said to have the highest magnetic frequency of all flowers. Red rose is for passion and white rose is for compassion.

I drink this potion after an argument or when grief hits my heart.

WHAT YOU'LL NEED

Blender
Saucepan

INGREDIENTS

1 mug of plant milk (whatever mug
   you will be drinking from)
1½ teaspoons maca powder
1 teaspoon coconut sugar
a pinch of ground cloves
¼ teaspoon ground ginger
¼ teaspoon ground cinnamon
a pinch of vanilla powder or
   a drop of pure vanilla extract
a pinch of cayenne pepper
a sprinkle of chopped dried rose petals,
   to finish

METHOD

Heat the plant milk in a saucepan over a medium heat (do not bring to the boil), then add the rest of the ingredients (except the rose petals), whisking together until hot and well combined.

Pour into a blender and blitz for 30 seconds, then pour into your mug and finish with a sprinkle of rose petals.

A TONIC FOR THE NIGHT AFTER

Makes: 1 mug   Time: 5 minutes

We have all had wild nights, when we wake up and feel a little rough. Usually a lot of fun was had, but the next day does not feel that fun. I realized that I needed a tonic to help soothe and refresh my body and pump it with goodness. I used to make my own activated charcoal from coconut skin, but I think your best bet is to buy it. Activated charcoal powder can be found in all health shops.

Coconut water is full of electrolytes, which help us to hardcore hydrate. Activated charcoal powder helps to cleanse the body of things that don't serve us. Lime juice is a refreshing element and helps to balance any acidity in the body. The power of plants to the rescue!

I give this to anyone with a hangover, or who has been up all night on the hard stuff. I also make it when I'm travelling in India, and, well, there's a disco happening in my belly. Best first thing in the morning.

INGREDIENTS
250ml/9fl oz/1 cup cold coconut water
1 teaspoon agave syrup
1 teaspoon activated charcoal powder
1 tablespoon lime juice

METHOD
Stir everything together well until all combined. Serve.

MOON JAM POTION

Makes: 1 mug   Time: 20 minutes

For me, when the full moon and new moon appear, it's time to take a pause and reflect and connect with myself more deeply. The ever-changing moon is a reminder that we are cyclical beings. The moon affects water, and we are 70 per cent water, so are affected by it too. I believe we all have an innate connection to nature and its cycles, and by using the moon as a guide, it has helped me bring more harmony and presence to my life.

A new moon is to set intentions. Every month on the new moon, I sit and think about what I want to create in the next 28 days, how I want to feel and what I want to bring into my life. The full moon is a celebration of what was/has been and what is, what I want to let go of, a time of feasting and connecting with my tribe.

My grandma would often talk about sitting in circle, drinking herbal delights. A place where people can come together and share. Our ancestors have been doing this all over the world for years. So I created moon jams. We drink my moon jam potion, read poetry, share, sing, laugh and sometimes even have a little cry. We learn about what flowers and plants are in season, what this means in folklore, how the seasons are changing and how that affects our moods. I have seen many people arrive in their head and leave in their heart.

In Colombia, when I lived on a cacao farm, the caretakers of the cacao plants would pick the beans by hand, roast them in the sun and grind them to a paste with their hands. We would drink cacao daily for energy and to connect to this delicious plant. Everything about this plant and its process is a ceremony. We didn't have cacao ceremonies on the farm because, for the indigenous, life is the ceremony; it isn't something that can be brought or glamourized. It is a way of life – how they connect and use the cacao and other plants was part of their daily practise. The plant is medicine that should be respected. It's a sacred fruit and known as the fruit of the gods.

Cacao has indeed assisted in opening my heart. When I arrived on the farm, my heart was so closed, I didn't even want to drink the cacao. I would avoid it; there was so much resistance in me. Every night, Titio (uncle) would tell me to have a little sip, and I would politely decline. He would tell me stories of how this plant meets you where you are at, a medicine for the heart. One night by the fire, I had a sip, and it very quickly became a daily drink. Over the next 6 months I started to notice changes in me and around me. I realized it wasn't the cacao I was scared of, it was losing control once my heart started to open again. I was scared of meeting myself in places I have run from. I explained this to him and Titio laughed and said, "Hija, it warms where once was cold. You are ready to work with this plant ... you, cacao and your cold heart have become friends."

We would sit by the fire and drink cacao, work on the land and drink cacao. We would sing to it. Hold it with love. Laugh with it. Be playful with it.

This potion is a blend of cacao to open the heart, with mugwort to connect to the dream world.

WHAT YOU'LL NEED
Saucepan

INGREDIENTS
1 mug of almond milk (whatever mug you will be drinking from)

30g/1oz cacao paste (if you don't have ceremonial cacao, you can use 4 tablespoons cacao powder)

1 teaspoon coconut sugar

1 tablespoon dried mugwort leaves

a pinch of cayenne pepper

METHOD
Heat the almond milk in a saucepan over a medium–low heat. Use a sturdy knife to flake or chop the cacao paste into small pieces. Add the cacao paste (or cacao powder if you are working with that), the coconut sugar, mugwort leaves and cayenne pepper. Heat for about 15 minutes, stirring regularly to ensure there are no lumps. Singing as you stir is optional but is a good way to connect with the plants and bring more love into your potion.

Once ready to serve, remove the mugwort leaves with a spoon. Enjoy under a full or new moon.

REFLECTIONS

In all honesty, I put off writing this book for years. People would ask where they can find my recipes and I would say a book is coming, knowing full well I hadn't even started writing it. It was all in my head. It wasn't just gonna be recipes, it was my journey, and I think I wasn't quite ready to share that until now.

Really deep down I didn't believe I could actually write a book; I always thought it was for people who had been to uni or were really good at spelling. Not someone like me. That's the thing with fear: it can hold you back from doing the very thing you want to do. But I've finally done it, stepped into the fear, and here it is in your hands.

For me, it's all about the storytelling around the food and the connection that happens through sharing food. I have learned that sharing openly with my heart is the only way I can truly live. Some stories may have resonated; maybe some seemed out there. But I hope that they have brought some comfort and maybe even inspired you. I hope that you've taken what you want from the book and let it hit you where it needed to.

It's up to us to build a community; there is so much separation in the world, yet I do believe that sharing a potion or a plant feast, being courageous and opening our hearts, being vulnerable and having deeper conversations not only connects us, but can be the start of a revolution that begins right from the dinner table ... genius or mad, I'll let you decide.

To be honest, this book has been nostalgic to write; it has taken me to places that I haven't thought about in a while. Perhaps I wasn't even ready to process what a wild journey I've been on, am still on.

Each recipe in this book I created from the heart, with love. I hope you create some plant magic too.

Channel the alchemist inside you.

Try dancing all night with the Stay Up Till Sunrise potion.

Make a recipe, make a few, be playful in the kitchen and invite friends, lovers or even people you just met to share them with you.

But most importantly, make ceremony for yourself.

Get to know your local plants and connect with the seasons. If you think you can't cook, if I can learn, you can too (I was shit in the beginning).

As with all things in life, you just gotta give it a go.

On a level, though, thank you for buying my book.

My mum was right all along: people and society will try and put you in a box and it's up to you to burn it. I have a million characters inside of me ... don't we all?

Being seen for who we really are is a powerful thing, but how can people know how epic we are, who we really are, if we don't show them?

Stay true to you; eat more plants, however that is for you.

Life is the ceremony.

ACKNOWLEDGEMENTS

Mum, our relationship has been a journey, and over time I have realized the things that I found hard to love about you were in fact the very things I found hard to love within me. Thank you for showing me that it's not what you don't have; it's what you do with what you got, not only in life but with ingredients too. Your open heart inspires me. Thank you for showing me that speaking your truth, even when it's uncomfortable – in fact especially when it's uncomfortable – is the only way to live. I don't tell you enough how grateful I am. Con, my step dad, fair play for taking on two teenagers and my wild mum. Every day you show me how humans can be soft and strong and that is the only way to really show up in this world.

Hannah, it's true that soul mates come in the form of friends. Thank you for all your beautiful photos; this book would not have been written without you giving me a kick up the arse and reminding me to get out of my own damn way! Thank you for always taking the time to read through my words, supporting me and being up for all the random adventures over the last 20 years. We're so blessed that we still create together, and this time we get paid for it ... maybe the hustle is finally starting to pay off!

Of course, big thanks to my nan – you've been dropping seeds of wisdom since day one; it just took me a while to hear you. Thank you for reminding me to make time as I get older to still see the magic in the world and connect with plants daily. It's this that keeps you young and keeps you so playful. Thank you for reminding me that when we lose a loved one they are never gone; they are speaking to us through the wind and tress, that they came from nature and return to nature.

Big thank you Sabrina, Priya and Madaline for always offering your home to me when I'm in need. Priya, I will never understand your love for full stops ... even after writing a book it just ruins my flow. Charlotte, thank you for the floor jams, feasts and critiques and always being up for all my random ideas.

To my crew dem who remind me that freedom is in the mind. You have always been open to all the different characters I have been along the way and continue to allow space for me to grow. Supporting all my events, believing in my vision and my food and reminding me I'm not mad. There are so many of you to name but you know who you are. I appreciate you and love you, and I feel blessed to have you in my life. Thank you guys for being my chosen family, encouraging my dreams and for your never ending support.

Naz, my agent, you're just epic. Thank you for keeping me grounded with your earthy energy; this book wouldn't exist without you. I am so grateful you came into my life.

To the whole team at Watkins, thank you for not squashing who I am and helping me turn my dream into a reality. To Ella for saying yes to sharing my story and my art, and to

Brittany and Karen for helping me birth *Plant Feasts* into the world. Also thank you for being so patient with me.

To my Latin family for reminding me that all emotions are valid and passion lives in everything! Thank you for holding me while I started to remember who I am.

To all the humans that have come to my meals, moon jams, storytelling around the fire, workshops and retreats, thank you. I fee humbled and inspired by you. You remind me to create and open my heart more. And big thanks to all who helped support and be part of moody mango. Jenny, we dreamed those supper clubs from my tiny one bedsit.

To my hairdressing clients for their support and love. Know I really appreciate you guys.

To Clare and Lee organics team and the city farms across London, thank you for showing me that you can learn about the earth and how things grow even in a city. That we can focus on the buildings or take time to learn the trees.

And of course thank you to my readers for choosing to buy and read my book – I appreciate all of you!

And a little thank you to me. I made a hard decision years ago to get off the drugs and change my life. It's funny because I thought it was the drugs that gave me freedom. Nah I now see that its sitting in the uncomfortable and connecting with nature that has given me a freedom I didn't even know was possible.

INDEX

NOTE: PAGE NUMBERS IN BOLD REFER TO ILLUSTRATIONS.